THE GOSPEL OF GOD

by

HERBERT KELLY

Founder of the Society of the Sacred Mission,
Kelham

WITH A MEMOIR BY
BROTHER GEORGE EVERY, SSM

SCM PRESS LTD

First published 1959
by the SCM Press Ltd, 56 *Bloomsbury Street, London, WC*1

© SCM PRESS LTD 1959

Set in Monotype Caslon
and printed in Great Britain by
The Bowering Press, Plymouth

CONTENTS

The frontispiece photograph is of the bronze bust of H. H. Kelly at the House of the Sacred Mission, Kelham.

FOREWORD

AFTER World War I, two student generations were vouch-safed the religious leadership of giants—such as were John Mott, 'T' himself, J. H. Oldham, Neville Talbot, William Temple. In the background always, and sometimes on the platform, was the *Eminence Grise*, Father Herbert Kelly. Already becoming a legendary figure he was then, as always, *mysterium fascinans*—challenging attention in any context and defying any conventional classification. His habit revealed him as some kind of 'monk'—which made him seem only the more alarming. But whenever he spoke, and even when he didn't, the spell he wielded was irresistible. It was on that terrain that I first came under it—in those years I had some contact with students. Much later in life it is now my privilege to hold office as Visitor of Kelham—that seminal thought of his which was made flesh. But it was at Swanwick that we saw Kelly plain. And this book, as Bro. George Every's memoir tells us, grew out of some lectures which he delivered there. It may fairly be taken to summarize his teaching, and phrase after phrase reminds one, re-reading it, how exciting and how pregnant that was. Indeed we are only now beginning to realize how profound and penetrating was his influence.

Mr Colin Wilson remarked that *The Outsider* was 'not an attempt to prove the existence of God but a search for meaning in human life'. Compare that with the opening paragraph of the Preface (p. 41) and you see how down to date Kelly's thinking was. It was indeed a long way ahead of his time. Like his acknowledged master, F. D. Maurice, he was far more prophet than system-maker, and in fact he distrusted theological systems. At a time when few anglican theologians were asking the ultimate questions at all, Fr Kelly was driving back to the fundamentals. 'It is possible that we have missed "theology" and are only studying "theological subjects".' He was always asking the theological questions—Does God do anything? What is human life and what does it say to us or do with us?

For God meets us first of all in the facts of life, and that is where theology must begin. An American Bishop has said that 'to love God is to submit to reality in its ultimate form': that is pure Kelly. 'God and religion are not quite the same thing'; and nobody who sat at 'the old man's feet can avoid putting the word 'religion' in quotes!

This existential approach to theology ('if you want proof of the Resurrection come and look at my pigs') was what guided his whole method of ordination training.

Today when the theological education so badly needs revision and reassessment how much the Church can still learn from his vision. This way of starting from life situations, rather than *a priori* assertion, is not at the moment in favour with theologians, yet it is, I am certain, what laymen need and what their clergy ought to be trained to give them. And Father Kelly may soon come into his own again. He would not, perhaps, 'go down' with a modern audience. His language, his manner and his idiosyncrasies (some of which are evident in the book) may date him too much.

But he is a prophet for this generation.

This great man has never been given his due. The centenary of his birth in 1960 has seemed to the Community an occasion to reintroduce him to the post-war reader and to pay tribute to his memory by the republication of this book. Alike on grounds of personal gratitude and in my more official capacity (the Director being at present overseas) I am glad to be asked to write this foreword to it.

RUSSELL SOUTHWELL

Bishop's Manor, Southwell
Christmas 1958

FATHER KELLY

I T was getting dark in the big tent at Swanwick. Outside it was still light on the first evening of the second summer conference and camp of the Student Christian Movement in July 1927, when we heard the address that was afterwards expanded into this book, first published in 1928. I well remember this, for this was the first meeting of my first conference, as well as my first contact with Father Kelly. On the platform stood a tall, gaunt figure, with white hair, who looked immensely old. Outlined against the canvas of the tent his silhouette seemed more like mediaeval sculpture than any man of the modern world. The secretaries were worried. 'The old man' was to be launched for the first time on the whole body of the young. For nearly twenty years he had been about in the wings, sitting on the stairs with secretaries and lecturers, sometimes speaking in parallel courses, letting out provocative aphorisms which could never be completely forgotten, to which the staff of the Movement, and a circle of senior friends, were constantly forced to return. But a lecture full of these, punctuated with pauses and 'gee-whiz', might be very imperfectly intelligible.

It was better than they expected. I have looked again at what was reproduced in the *Quarterly Paper* of the Society of the Sacred Mission in the next September.[1] This begins:

'We are met in the most holy name of Religion. I am not quite sure what people mean by that somewhat heathen word (never used of Christianity in the New Testament), but my business is to talk about God, which is not quite the same thing.'

[1] Vol. 27, no. 100, September 1927, pp. 70–8.

So far as I can remember (and I was there) what he really said was, 'I am going to talk to you about God. Some of you think that means religion, which is not quite the same thing.' A little later he said, 'Let us face this thought of God. The ultimate will has reality first as power. . . . Some clever people who know philosophy insist that reality is value. I am not clever, and my stupidity can make nothing of it. The war, a total eclipse at six a.m., a forgotten tent-peg in the dark, really *are* whether you have any value for them or not. Values do not make things.'

In those days we were all idealists. I do not mean that we knew or understood anything much about absolute idealism, as it was taught in the philosophical schools, but we believed that the world we knew was shaped by human purposes, that it was a great improvement on the world of nature, and that it could and would be 'moulded nearer to our heart's desire.' The first great war had made very little difference to these expectations, except to intensify them. The League of Nations and the World Revolution both offered hopes of a new world, 'made safe for democracy', in one or the other version of the same. The tension between them could be represented as growing pains, as the like tension between East and West to-day cannot be. Only very lately in 1926 the long continuance of industrial disputes that arose out of the General Strike, and of unemployment, had made us wonder whether here in England our own national problem was soluble, whether we might have come to the end of our greatness, and be obliged to resign ourselves to a decline in our standard of life.

Father Kelly had long been asking questions like these, that now flowed from the platform: 'What does God do? Does God do anything, or is God only another name for ideals? Is God's purpose something which God is doing, is carrying out, or only something which he would very much

10

like us to have, but which he is powerless to effect, and wishes you would do for him?' He spoke of 'the world force, the ultimate of all thinking, which in the end disposes of all that man proposes', and then of 'the religious side of our craving to escape the world-problem. . . . Pure religion, undefiled by theology, is personal, concerned with the self, its states, feelings, and experiences. I think the cult of religion always ends there.'

'But all religions begin here:

'Men have always believed there was a God, because the world was intelligible and good.

'On the other hand, men have believed *in* God, because the world wasn't intelligible, and so much of it seemed evil.'

That rang a bell, every bell. The whole was leading on to the conclusion: 'Realize this first, that your life . . . is not your own; accept it so, and when faith meets hope, love is born.' To 'accept the universe' may seem a queer kind of conversion. No doubt we accept it first, because there is no way else. We cannot make universes. But to 'accept it so', with the quality of hope, is much more than to grin and bear it. It is to turn a forced acquiescence in the grain of things into 'faith working through love'. Like so many others, I had hoped to transform the grain of things after my desires. I had believed in goodness and value, and in the goodness and value of religion and religious ideas, but shuddered at their association in theological language with 'being, power, and truth', with 'God the Father Almighty, maker of heaven and earth'. Now I began to glimpse that 'we have just got to learn them as they are', not as we should like them to be. That meant God's ways, and not only God's ways in religion, but also heaven and earth as he has made them, life and death as they really are.

How did Father Kelly himself begin to see this?

Herbert Hamilton Kelly was born on 18th July 1860, one of a large family in Lancashire parsonages. The boys went to Manchester Grammar School, and so were spared the separations characteristic of their class in their age. The family always remained very closely knit. So long as his mother lived, she was Herbert's most intimate correspondent, and for much in the early history of his foundation, the Society of the Sacred Mission, his letters to her are the chief authority. His youngest brother joined the Society, and one of his sisters the Community of the Epiphany. I remember his eldest brother, a brigadier-general, on the platform of a meeting of the English Church Union in the West of England. But the family background was Evangelical. Herbert was originally intended for the artillery, and got as far as Woolwich and a commission, but the beginnings of deafness and a growing seriousness in his religious convictions led him to resign his commission as soon as it was obtained. In October 1880 he went up to Queen's College, Oxford, as an ordinand. His Oxford career was academically undistinguished. He emerged with a third class in mathematical moderations, and with fourth-class honours in history in the final schools, but more happened at Oxford besides examinations and awards. He discovered Charles Kingsley, the Kingsley of *Madam How and Lady Why* (a book that always remained one of his classics). Through Kingsley, he found F. D. Maurice, and learnt from him: 'That God is not the same as religion; that the church and sacraments were also realities, far greater than our theories about them; that the theories, even negative theories, were witnessing to positive realities.'

In an autobiographical sketch of his 'personal thoughts concerning unity',[1] he went on to say: 'This led me to share Maurice's distrust for authoritarian and verbal orthodoxies.

[1] Typescript of September 1927, at Kelham.

I did share his reverence for authority, but as I remember saying, "It is a guide to thinking, not a substitute for it. Faith . . . is a faith in God, not in doctrines. In the end, you will have to find what the doctrines mean to you." '

Kingsley and Maurice laid him open to Catholic influences when they freed him from the Protestant prejudices associated with Evangelical piety, but—

'I knew no one worth knowing in Catholic circles, and the few I did know were not very helpful, since to them "the authority of the Church" was always apt to mean a series of doctrines stated by a recognized authority. The idea of the Catholic Church and of Catholic authority made an immense appeal to me. It was a vision of a great, whole, ordered, common truth—wherein men at all times lived. . . . Certainly the phrase "Scripture as interpreted by Catholic consent" seemed to come as near the truth as any phrase can. I would never separate myself from that consent, but Pusey's apparent belief that the teaching of God's Spirit could be fixed in a catena of consentual extracts seemed to me to break down in fact as it does in principle. I could never be Roman, because that theory is a formal substitution (vicariate) of another process for the living God. I am a learner. I wanted to learn from an eternal Spirit of all ages—primitive, mediaeval, modern—the self-same Spirit.'

Dr Pusey was still alive when he went up to Oxford, and still the dominant influence in the Anglo-Catholic movement, but among the younger Anglo-Catholic dons dangerous thoughts were stirring, which a few years later would find expression in *Lux Mundi* (1889). The group represented there would come to terms with modern philosophy and Biblical criticism, and present the religion of the incarnation as directly relevant to the social problems of modern England. Only one of them, Scott Holland, a student of Christ Church until 1884, and then a canon of St Paul's, had any direct personal influence on Father Kelly, who was never satisfied with *Lux Mundi*. He wrote in later years (1906)[1] that 'It is too evidently of the nature of a compromise to affect the situation very deeply. It well recognizes that there are two elements which want recognizing, and those who are not inclined to think very deeply or who have given it up in despair may be content. Few genuine thinkers however are likely to be satisfied with unresolved antinomies, or with balance for its own sake.'

The criticism applies not only to *Lux Mundi*, but to a great deal in the writings of Bishop Gore, and to much in the Liberal Catholic approach to the problems of reconciling modern philosophy with Catholic tradition. Herbert Kelly's thinking was too genuine to be easily satisfied with a synthesis of conclusions without an examination of the methods whereby those conclusions were reached. This habit of mind was established in him before he left Oxford. It was probably responsible for his academic failures. He did not go to Cuddesdon, where Gore was vice-principal then, but straight on to be ordained deacon in the diocese of Canterbury. His first curacy was at Leeds, a Kent village (1883–6), and his second at St Paul's, Wimbledon Park. In both the churchmanship was moderate.

'In those days', he wrote at the end of his life,[2] 'the 1880's, when curates were much more common than they are now, every part of the Church, notably the mission field, was crying out for men. Where were they to come from? Those recruited through the usual channels were insufficient to meet the new demands. In my second curacy, in south London, I tried to do what I could with the boys in the poor district of South-

---

[1] *Ad fratres*, privately circulated to the brethren.
[2] *SSM Quarterly Paper*, vol. 51, no. 177, December 1950 (posthumous).

fields. It seemed to me that the Church could find the men she needed from such as these, if only the necessary education could be provided. I went to Scott Holland, the only man I knew among the big people, and suggested that if a free college were started, with no half-baked gentility—we might get quite a number, but who was I to start anything? He said it was coming, but not yet. . . . I was ready to give myself, and what money I had, for anything.'

At that time the Church of England did not seem to be interested in offers of service from anyone who had not been at the proper public schools and the older universities, though something was being said of a shortage of clergy and of the possibility of using men with less education in the mission field or in difficult industrial parishes.

Nearly all those who were trying to tackle this problem still took for granted the general educational and social standards of the period. It was admitted that men might be used whose background did not include preparation for the university, and that finance was a difficulty, but the general assumption was that whatever was done would be on the lines of a cheaper and easier version of a pass degree at Oxford, Cambridge, or Durham. 'Because the men were uneducated, the intellectual side must be simplified as much as possible. A few simple text-books giving the . . . essential facts or doctrines, must be got up. For explanations the student, unaccustomed to reading, must depend mainly on his lectures. That he shall know at least the main facts, know which are the correct doctrines, and the reasons for them, is all you can expect. . . . The one thing which really matters is the sincerity of the devotional life.'[1] This approach was common to nearly all Anglicans, Evangelical as well as Anglo-Catholic, concerned with raising the standard of training for the

[1] Typescript of September 1927, at Kelham.

15

priestly life at this time, partly perhaps because of uneasy anxieties at the growing secularity of the universities. The Free Churches, who had only lately acquired opportunities for study at Oxford and Cambridge, were more aware of the intellectual limitations of their ministers, and therefore more anxious for more theology.

Father Kelly's approach to the whole question was governed from the very first by theological principles. 'These men were going to be teachers of a faith, given in a creed. This is said to be correct, and that incorrect, but . . . I would rather ask, why is this doctrine vital, and that fatal, to a man's soul and capacity to live? Someone said it was, and he ought to know. Very well, we must go to him, and find out why he found it so; then each man must look into his own soul, find in his own life its questions and difficulties, its perplexities and diversities. . . . Prayer is meditation, and study is meditation, but God, the love of God, the following of God, is one. At a later stage we summarized it under the term "theological football". Here is a creed, a faith, a theology, a belief in God, and here is a boy's game. What have they to do with one another? Here is a cheese-factory, and here a cheese shop. Is God interested in the efficiency of our processes of manufacture and selling, or only in the morals of those who manufacture and sell? Surely, if God made the world, then our processes are efficient where they follow God's ways. If we split life into religious sections, moral sections, business sections, it is plain, God does not; nor does he make it possible for most people.' In the same note Father Kelly goes on to say: 'Theology I conceive to be the study of the vision, of the great life-purpose, and there is no ultimate purpose except in God. If our theology is unpractical, it is that view of life-purpose we have missed. It is possible we have missed "theology" and are only studying "theological subjects".

Then we had better get back. No doubt theology does need practice. Meditation, prayer, study, which all lead towards a vision of purpose; worship, scrubbing stairs, sweeping a passage, washing dishes, which flow from it, are all very appropriate practices at this stage, and useful at some other stages.'

'During 1890 I worked out in my head the idea of what I wanted, but I had no notion how or by whom it could be carried out. There were at that time three openings for . . . myself. One was in the north of England, another in Australia . . .; but the third was the most pressing. An ex-naval chaplain, Bishop Corfe, had been offered the bishopric of Korea, for which a big grant had been allotted. The intention was to do the job on the lines of . . . a common fund, no marriage, and a community mission.'[1] This was the most urgent, but the least attractive of the three, for Father Kelly believed himself 'much too stupid to learn a language, and much too full of ideas to be a useful missionary. However, I took the alternatives to Scott Holland, and asked him to make the choice. He told me to go to Korea—the one thing I did not want to do. But I had said it, and so I had to go.'

However he did tell Bishop Corfe something about his dreams, and the Bishop threw back his own problem on him. 'Here was a wonder: just as I gave it up, the whole idea was thrust back into my hand.' The Bishop had offers of service from a dozen young laymen. How could they be trained and prepared? To take them to Korea as they were was manifestly impossible. Through the instrumentality of Canon Brooke, the Bishop's commissary in England, who was vicar of St John's, Kennington, a house was found at 97, Vassall Road, where Father Kelly would train them, and any others who might come, not necessarily for the Korean mission. Of

[1] *SSM Quarterly Paper*, vol. 51, no. 177, December 1950 (posthumous).

the twelve who had offered, only one came, although two others soon joined them. The year 1891 was just beginning. By 1894 the Korean missionary brotherhood had become the Society of the Sacred Mission, at first designed to strengthen the work of two existing missions, the mission to Korea and the Universities' Mission to Central Africa, both working on Anglo-Catholic lines. The connection with Central Africa lasted for many years, and a link still remains in one member of the Society at work in the diocese of Zanzibar. The Korean province came to an end earlier, although Father Henry John Drake, SSM, returned to the Korean mission and worked there for many years between the wars, and indeed until the Japanese intervened in the Second World War and interned the missionaries. Another member of the Society is now assistant secretary of the mission, which has of late years received recruits from among the old students of Kelham. The SSM developed a life of its own through its ventures in education, and after a time found another mission, not only in the Orange Free State and in Basutoland, but in the training of clergy for labour in English parishes and in missions not under its own direction, first at Mildenhall (1898–1903), then at Kelham from 1903 onwards, and since 1947 also on Mount Lofty, near Adelaide in South Australia.

Kelham is now chiefly known as a unique instrument of education, but this was a by-product of theology and the Society. Father Kelly's original intention was to train a small band of men, and probably go with them to the Far East. Out of the failure of this, or its limited success, the idea rose to the surface of his mind of an order as wide as the Church and the world, with provinces in three continents and possibly independent divisions in America and Australia. That this idea had long been incubating beneath the surface is suggested by the range of ground covered in the detailed provisions of the first constitution of 1894. Much of this has inevitably been superseded, but the idea stands. Nevertheless expansion on the expected scale has never taken place. In the original design it was anticipated that all who came for training and survived testing would make profession of their intention to serve for life under obedience in the Society of the Sacred Mission. Some did, and some did not. Not all of those who did persevered. It soon became obvious that there must be a place in the House of the Sacred Mission for 'associates' who wished to receive their training with the Society, as well as for novices preparing for profession and life-membership.[1] After a few years associates outnumbered novices. They are now to be found all over the world. They include an Australian archbishop, a distinguished Cambridge theologian, many missionaries, and an SCM secretary.

In the early days no doubt the attraction of training at Mildenhall and at Kelham lay primarily if not entirely in the opportunity of austerity and religious discipline, in preparation for tasks, in the mission field and in England, whose starkness and difficulty were beginning to be appreciated. Anglicans were just beginning to perceive that to be a 'gentleman' is not in itself a sufficient qualification for a clergyman. But before long another attraction presented itself, the opportunity of a thorough grounding in theology over four years. In about 1900 this was something so extraordinary as to be scandalous in the Church of England, where theological colleges were still commonly regarded as an expedient for the partial education of literates who could not or did not graduate at one of the universities. 'In 1874, only a small proportion of the

[1] 'An Associate is a member of a house of the Society who, in sympathy with its principles and aims, has expressed a desire to consecrate his life to the service of God's Church and has promised obedience to the Rule and Superiors of the house while he remains a member of it' (SSM current 'Information for candidates').

graduate ordinands went on to a theological college, though it was increasing; and if they did go there, they might only stay for a term or two. Others went to live with a clergyman for a few months before their ordination, reading the subjects of their diocesan examination, and gaining a little experience of parish work under his guidance. Some would remain at their university for one or more or additional terms, attending the lectures of the divinity professors, and sharing in the religious life of their college and of the university generally, but, as a rule, thrown more or less on their own resources. . . . Many others went simply to their own homes, and did as they or their parents thought fit. Residence at the university and obtaining a degree were regarded by the majority as an adequate training.'[1] It is unlikely that the position in 1894 was radically different. The number of graduates who went for a year or more to Cuddesdon had increased, but not dramatically. Father Kelly himself was not among them, though his younger brother was. The proportion of non-graduates had also increased, and among them the number who had attended a theological college for two or more years. But very little had yet been done to provide them with more than an inexpensive substitute for university education.

The English idea of theology in the 1890's was limited to Scriptural exegesis and some acquaintance with the controversies and councils of the early Church and the Christian fathers. Neither the Evangelical nor the Tractarian movements had produced theologians in the sense of powerful thinkers;[2] and the Liberal theologians, though some of them

[1] F. W. B. Bullock, *A History of Training for the Ministry*, St Leonard's, 1955, p. 147.
[2] No doubt exceptions might be cited on both sides, but on the side that I know best it seems to me that the most powerful theological minds either became Roman Catholic, like Newman and R. I. Wilberforce, or like J. B. Mozley, diverged from Tractarian positions, or like Charles Marriott, left little written.

were thinkers of very considerable speculative power, were more concerned with religious experience and with the interpretation of religious ideas than with the unknown and unknowable, the incomprehensible God. Many of them eschewed all concern with metaphysical speculation and would confine their religious thinking to the values of the Christian life. F. D. Maurice had soared above this, and Westcott and Hort with him. Scott Holland was one of those who had something of Maurice in him, and this may well have been the root of his sympathy for an ungainly curate with ill-expressed Maurician ideas. Father Kelly constantly insisted that he was the only person of weight who took any notice of him. But by and large the Anglo-Catholic movement was not much concerned with theology in the 1890's.

Anglo-Catholics were concerned either with the persistence of the ritualistic revival in liturgical worship, or with social ethics and the possibility of synthesis between aspirations after social reconstruction and religious tradition. It was Maurice the socialist who won a kind of grudging recognition for Maurice the theologian. Bishop Gore and Father James Adderley are the representative figures of this period. Neither of them ever quite understood Father Kelly, or his idea of theology. His interest in the scholastic theologians, and his desire for a complete course in philosophy and theology, to be developed on other lines than those of the universities, suggested something like a Roman Catholic seminary, and for a time won some sympathy from the conservative and anti-critical wing of the Anglo-Catholic party. But then Father Kelly disappointed and surprised them by making friends with the Student Christian Movement and appearing at Baslow in 1908, and in 1910 at the Edinburgh Conference, where the Society for the Propagation of the Gospel did not dare to be represented.[1] Interdenominational movements were then suspected, not only by the extremists, but by many Liberal Anglo-Catholics. But Father Kelly was at Edinburgh, talking theology with Scottish Presbyterians. Soon afterwards, he published *The Church and Religious Unity* (1913), his first formidable contribution to the discussion of the ecumenical problem.

What was and is really distinctive about 'Kelham theology' is not a matter of conclusions, of a theological position, but of a concern. At no time was Father Kelly an original theologian. He was simply a theological student at a time when nearly all other Anglicans (but not all Scotsmen, or Germans, or Roman Catholics) were concerned about other things. They were concerned with the study of theological ideas considered as part of a religion, or of a series of religions, the religions of the Old and New Testaments, of Catholic Christendom, of the Reformation. Father Kelly was concerned with the knowledge of God and his works, with 'what God does', with whether, as he was always asking, 'God is big or little', with the meaning of the incarnation, 'not by the conversion of the Godhead into flesh but by taking of the manhood into God', 'the Father incomprehensible, the Son incomprehensible, and the Holy Ghost incomprehensible'. In an age when most theologians were concerned either with 'the varieties of religious experience', or with the correct definitions, he directed the attention of his students to the unrepresented, to all that cannot be said about God, to the

[1] See H. P. Thompson, *Into all Lands, the History of the SPG, 1701–1950*, London, 1951, p. 487: 'The SPG refused to be officially represented, and the Conference . . . was not even mentioned in its report of 1910. But Bishop Montgomery himself [the Secretary] and Mrs Creighton were on the preparatory Committees, and thirty-four members unofficially represented the SPG and made their full contribution. Yet not until 1918 did the Society join the Conference of British Missionary Societies.' See also G. K. A. Bell, *Randall Davidson*, Oxford, 1935, vol. ii, p. 797, for the general Anglican attitude at the time.

infinity of reality and the failure of all our words to discover or to describe what God does.

This emphasis was deepened by the course of events. The students were not all particularly brilliant or discerning. The Society did not develop according to the first plan. To direct operations in Korea from Kennington or Mildenhall proved impossible, or at that stage to divide authority and preserve unity. At Mildenhall and in the early years at Kelham (from 1903) there were many setbacks and disappointments, but the vision remained, and the conviction of a mission, not a personal mission for Father Kelly, but a mission for the Society which some day would be (and, please God, will be) accomplished more completely. That depended all the time on vocations, on 'reasons hidden in the will of God'. Father Kelly was excessively anxious that his Society should not be 'a one-man show'. In 1910 when the General Chapter was equally divided on the question of accepting his resignation, his own determination was decisive. He wished to go further, to seek release and re-enter as a novice, without precedence.

The reasons for this were partly constitutional. It was not easy, in any case, to act on an even vote, but he maintained that:

'The proceeding corresponds faithfully to the true state of the case. It is not merely a technical difficulty we have to evade. The real difficulty springs from the fact that I have— at least in the eyes of the Church—allowed my own personality to overshadow the real power of the Society. If the Society had been unanimous in her desire for a new Director, that would have proved that she was free from that error. But her opinion is not unanimous. If I persuade some delegates here to change their votes, the Society will have reached a decision which will be loyally accepted. But that is not suffi-cient. . . . It is merely giving in to my strong views. It is

23

another Kelly theory. You may have uses for me presently, but just now you want to get rid of me entirely. What good is it if you choose a new captain, as long as I remain sitting in an easy chair on the quarter-deck?

'To have ideas, to be able to explain them to students, is the business of a teacher. . . . I had plans. I have mapped them out and explained them. Everyone has heard everything I have to say and is tired of it. . . . My abilities and short-comings were excellently summed up by a certain member of a committee on which I had urged a certain policy. Of course the committee did not accept it; but the archdeacon said, "Fr Kelly's speech was extremely interesting. It has made me think." I consider that an achievement on my part of which few men are capable, but there it is. I can make people think; I cannot get them to do anything. . . . I am a staff college lecturer, not a commander.'

In the next ten years he spent much of his time away from Kelham. In March and April 1912 he went with Neville Talbot to the United States and Canada. At that time the YMCA in America were engaged with the Student Christian Movement in the British Isles and like movements on the continent of Europe in the development of the World's Student Christian Federation, and also in the expansion of the YMCA's own activities in South America, Eastern Europe, and the near East. In all this the central figure was the indefatigable John R. Mott, a universal traveller with more sensitiveness to all that he saw than might easily be imagined by a cursory reader of his biography.[1] He was well aware of the choice before Christian youth movements in Roman Catholic and Orthodox countries, either a reconcili-ation at some time and in some way with the ecclesiastical

[1] Basil Mathews, *John R. Mott, World Citizen.*

hierarchy, or a sectarian opposition that must cut them off from the life of their nation. The road to peace with Rome was at the moment formidably barred by the aftermath of the Modernist controversy, which had made Roman Catholics extremely afraid of dangerous thoughts and lay Christian movements. But the prospects in Russia and elsewhere in the Orthodox East were happier and seemed likely to improve in 1912, when the Czardom was expected to evolve into a liberal regime. There at least Episcopalian assistance could be of the first importance. It must be shown that the YMCA was not necessarily Protestant. The ostensible object of Father Kelly's mission was to persuade the American Episcopalians, and especially the Episcopalian theological colleges, to co-operate with the YMCA in the American universities.

In this the results were disappointing. Father Kelly was not a man to sway quickly or easily the upper circle of American Episcopalian society, or to induce it to overlook what must have seemed repulsive in down-town YMCAs reproduced on the campus. The real interest of the expedition lies in fresh friendships made with those High Church Episcopalians who were then beginning to plan the World Conference on Faith and Order, and in conversation with Mott, who had persuaded the YMCA to finance the journey. The reason for his choice of emissaries was not at first very obvious, but it gradually came out in the course of conversation that he wanted the Episcopalians in his movement not only for their social prestige, or for a diplomatic advantage in dealing with the Orthodox, but for the theology of the Church and sacraments, for something that he had seen growing in the British Student Christian Movement under Father Kelly's influence, the beginnings of a path across the gulf between Protestant and Catholic, and also something that might supply the element of objective authority that was disappearing from

25

American Protestantism with the evacuation of the old belief in the infallibility of the Scriptures.

At that time the whole movement for missionary collaboration, inspired by Mott's own slogan, 'the evangelization of the world in this generation', must have looked superficial, and complacently liberal, to any orthodox theologian. Plenty of hot air was certainly blowing about in missionary circles in America and Britain, and as Father Kelly was to see shortly, the air was even hotter in Japan. To see and feel this was comparatively easy. It was harder to see behind it a movement of the Spirit that would outlast the decay of liberal theology. *The Church and Religious Unity*, written in 1912 and published in 1913, is in some respects a dated book, but in others it is literally prophetic, in that it anticipates the future problems and interests of the ecumenical movement in a way that was altogether unusual at this time, when very few enthusiasts for Christian reunion were theologians, and very few theologians had any flexibility in their dealings with ecclesiastical problems.

As remarkable is a paper on *The Object and Method of Conference*, published, after revision, by the Faith and Order Committee in 1915, which surveys, with a truly remarkable acumen, the probable obstacles to beginning any real theological discussion between the several confessions, and how these are to be overcome, and the path plotted from controversy to conference. To a great extent these obstacles have been overcome. To read this pamphlet is to measure the extent of our limited, but important achievement through forty years of ecumenical conferences. It is well that we should remember how much we owe to the few who in preliminary conversations plotted the issues, and in particular to two whose deafness demanded that they should follow the other man's argument with the closest attention, lest a link escape them. It is not easy to discover how deaf Father Kelly was when he first began to attend conferences, though he was clearly deaf enough to feel it as a handicap. But it can hardly be a pure coincidence that two deaf men have done so much for the quality of theological conversation, H. H. Kelly and J. H. Oldham. Another who might be added is Baron von Hügel.

When *The Church and Religious Unity* was published, Father Kelly was on the other side of the world. He sailed to Japan in January 1913, and remained there for six years until 1919, returning for a General Chapter and furlough in 1915–6. The Japanese episode has a curious importance for the whole history of his life. He was asked to help in starting a new theological college, which should also be a house of studies. He never learnt the language, and it is perhaps doubtful whether he ever understood the Japanese. 'They are supposed to be hard to understand; my impression is that they are hard to understand because they are much simpler than we are.' Somehow or other they understood him much better than his English contemporaries. His own notes[1] may be quoted:

'The position was comprehensible enough. Their character is astonishingly simple; their mental education is Buddhist, which gives them rather a . . . liking for abstract philosophy. Mentally, our people fed them with (SPG) High Church orthodoxies and forms which they accepted in a bewildered way, and with (CMS) evangelical orthodoxies which they also accepted, without understanding, for there are very few genuinely "evangelical" Japanese. The American Protestants fed them with Modernisms, resting on criticism and a distant backwash of Harvard Idealism. . . . They did not in the least know what it meant, but it was the latest thing; it looked

[1] Typescript, autobiographical, to 1919, written *c.* 1930, pp. 98, 101.

clever . . . superior to the orthodoxy of old-fashioned traditionalism. They were hungering for something solid which
they could understand.

'. . . I laughed at the fine language which attracted them
so much; imitated it, made them see its absurdity, and brought
them back to the plain issues of faith in the reality of God. . . .
Of course, they had explanations and arguments in crowds, but
real "meanings" in my sense of the word (whatever that may
be) were quite new to them. All sorts of people whom I had
never seen took up whatever ideas I had to give, quietly, in
their own fashion, as they could see their way—which was
just what I wanted—and no one said: What does Fr Kelly
mean?'

'Did they agree with me? It was part of my joy that I
never, but once, heard the word mentioned. . . . As a rule
they just wanted to learn as much as they could, which is
exactly what I always want to do myself. . . . I played the
same game on the American Protestants where I could, and
they also fell to it. They were desperately solemn about their
personality-worship, character-building, and so on. I made
fun of it, and they rocked with laughter. It speaks volumes
for their genuineness that no one, to my knowledge, took
offence at it. It was in Japan, I think, that I first really learnt
the power of laughing and making people laugh with you.
You must laugh at yourself first; it is a very good antiseptic
for vanity.'

In his American diary of 1912 Father Kelly somewhere
complains: 'When I get into these blanked pulpits . . . I can
no more keep off rhetorical fireworks than I can keep off
rocks when I see 'em. And for all solid purposes they are about
equally useful. Everybody is filled with admiration as they
watch you wriggling out of impossible positions. . . . The
wild cheers are given solely to what they take to be your

cleverness. What you mean goes for nothing.' He might not have written that after Japan. But it is probably true to say that his acceptance by the Japanese had something to do with an element in their spiritual history that never came his way. If he had known stories about the sages of Zen Buddhism, he would certainly have told them at Kelham, but in his time Mahayana and Zen were commonly regarded by Western orientalists as decadent forms of the higher religion, the Hinayana, of Ceylon and Burma. I once asked a Japanese priest why Father Kelly made such an impression in his country. The immediate answer was that he was a holy man. A sage, and therefore a saint, in the Zen Buddhist reckoning, is known by the quality of his hard questions. Those jokes and paradoxes which in the eyes of Scottish and American reviewers made Father Kelly's books and pamphlets a little less than serious, established him as a sage in Japanese eyes.

'There was never anything like this in my life', he wrote regretfully later.[1] 'For once I really could think I had been effective, and whether it really came to anything, of course I cannot tell. . . . It is no wonder that I long to go back, even though I am quite conscious that I ate as much jam as was good for my foolish soul—and a bit more. I suspect also that I was in Japan as long as was good for them. I am a memory. If I had stopped longer, I might . . . have become a bore. I came back to something quite different.'

In 1919–20 the prospects for Christian unity were superficially brighter than at any time before or after. Much interest was aroused in a scheme for the integration of particular Congregational churches with the Episcopal Church of the United States, a plan which Father Kelly defended, with some reservations, much to the indignation of some American Anglo-Catholics. Schemes of the same kind began to be dis-

[1] Ibid., p. 102.

cussed in many parts of the world, including India, nor were all the obstacles obvious as yet. On the other hand the position at Kelham was more difficult than at any other time in the Society's history.

The house at Kelham had been emptied of nearly all its students during the first two years of the first World War, when so many young men obeyed the call to volunteer, and went to fight and die in Flanders or Gallipoli. In 1916 the house was evacuated, and taken over by the Royal Engineers, while the remnant of the community, and a handful of students, took refuge at Mirfield. When they returned in 1918, the Kelham estate had been sold, and for a time it seemed most probable that the lease would not be renewed, and that the house might be sold to a higher bidder over the Society's head. Other difficulties, as might be expected, were found in re-assembling the scattered brethren, but after a time the skies cleared. By the end of 1920 the house and grounds belonged to the Society, and by 1925, under young and vigorous leadership, Father Kelly's children were able to look forward with some confidence to a period of reconstruction and expansion, material and spiritual, at home and abroad. The new chapel at Kelham, an acknowledged masterpiece of architecture and engineering, was begun in 1927, dedicated in 1928, and carried a stage further in 1939. At the same time the headquarters of the Society in South Africa, at Modderpoort in the Orange Free State, became an important centre for training teachers.

In all this Father Kelly was a counsellor, not a commander, a lecturer, not a superior. He still had to carry a very large part of the teaching programme, in philosophy and Christian doctrine as well as in the second half of the church history, from the thirteenth century. In matters of policy his counsel was always sought, though not always taken. The leaders at this time were only partly his own pupils. Others were university graduates whose connection with Kelham dated from just after he ceased to be Director, from the years between 1910 and the first World war, when, among others, Father R. H. Tribe, Father Stephen Bedale, and Father Gabriel Hebert first arrived. This was perhaps fortunate, in that their reverence for the Father founder as a teacher and a sage was not impeded by recollections of the time when the 'staff lecturer' was acting as the superior officer. As a teacher, he was still at the height of his power.

He continued to do most of the lecturing in philosophy and doctrine until he was over seventy, and half of the church history until 1934. He did not give up lecturing altogether until ten years later. By that time he was a very old man, but he remained receptive to new ideas to an astonishing degree. In the early thirties he was much occupied with Eddington and Jeans, and with the mysterious universe of the philosophy of science. When this ceased to be his concern he went on reading new books on the Reformation. In 1948 or 1949 I showed him a paper of my own in which I had used an old distinction of his between justification by faith alone in Luther, and justification only by faith in Cranmer. He would not allow it, for he had been convinced by Franz Hildebrandt's book *Melanchthon: Alien or Ally* (1946) that this was precisely the difference between Luther and Melanchthon, and that Cranmer, as might be expected, was on Melanchton's side. In 1949, when he was almost ninety, he made elaborate notes on R. G. Collingwood's *Idea of History*.

My own recollections of his lectures date for the most part from 1930–2. I doubt if they were very different at any time after 1920 and before 1934, when I took over the last part of the church history, not because his powers were failing, but because like so many senior lecturers, he had so much to say that he could never finish. Often he would begin with a name, Ockham for instance, and then digress for ten minutes on the divine will and our ideas of the relation of will to law. By a sudden leap he was back in the fourteenth century, discoursing on the administrative arrangements of the Avignon Papacy. Then he would stop and say 'See?' How many saw straightaway? I do not know. I was myself at some advantage through having read a certain amount of the history. Flashes might light a landscape for me while others were merely dazzled. On the other hand, I was burdened with much irrelevant knowledge, which kept me from remembering what was relevant in other subjects and in other lectures, in texts from the Scriptures and distant controversies, and Father Kelly's own stories. Father Kelly always expected, and sometimes obtained, the recollection of all that was relevant, and in the effort to do this minds were stretched to the uttermost.

At this time his reputation was enhanced by the beginning of a general theological revival. It was said, with much reason, that those who had learnt from him were better able to understand Karl Barth. His relation to Barth was and is rather easily misunderstood. Some interesting comment can be found in a letter from Canon Quick,[1] relating to this book:

'You and Barth both insist that "God is greater than religion", but what I find in your book and miss in Barth is the complementary insistence that "we can only understand our life by reference to a whole order of things", and that all must be intelligibly (tho' not of course within the compass of our intelligence) related to God. The trouble is that if you emphasize merely the "irrational", eschatological, transcendent, other-than-human and other-than-natural aspects of the Divine Being, you represent Him just as a tremendous irruptive cataclysmic force; and *for that very reason* confine Him

[1] August 4th, 1930, quoted by the kind leave of Mrs Quick.

after all to one section of experience, and render valueless in the end the distinction between "God" and "religion" from which you began. This is the snare into which Barth seems to me to fall.'

When F. R. Barry (afterwards Bishop of Southwell) compared him to Barth in an article in *The Guardian*, Father Kelly went down to the incinerator and found among discarded oddments there a serviceable piece of headgear which was known for three or four years as 'my Karl Barth hat', but this enthusiasm cooled. 'So far as I can understand,' he said to me some years later, 'Barth has no doctrine of creation.' Where they really agreed was in objections to natural theology and general revelation. In Father Kelly's eyes all theology was revealed, and all revelation was specific, but specific revelation was given in events, and not only in those events recorded in the Scriptures.

In a review of *The Gospel of God* in *The Student Movement* William Temple wrote: 'You won't always agree with Father Kelly; but you will always find it worth while to discover why you disagree, when you do. And if your experience is like mine has been for some twenty years, you will fail to find a good reason for disagreeing, and find, with some vexation, that you have got to agree after all.'

Father Kelly's influence on Archbishop Temple has been rightly noticed in connection with the twelfth of his Gifford lectures, on 'revelation and its mode', in *Nature, Man, and God*; here, for instance:[1]

The typical locus of revelation is not the mind of the seer but the historical event. And if the revelation is essentially an event or fact, then it can be perfectly definite, though it neither is nor can be exhaustively represented in propositions.

[1] 1st ed., London, 1934, p. 318.

33

Father Kelly certainly thought in this way not only about the crossing of the Red Sea and the resurrection of Christ, but about the eucharist and the episcopate. 'Not even transubstantiation', he said somewhere, 'can take the mystery out of a sacrament'.[1] But when he was cross-questioned about his own influence on Temple, he maintained that 'the greater portion of Christian history' was on the same side, that 'the tendency to look on the sacred books as strings of authoritative statements only came in with the growth of legalistic interests in the Western Church'[2] of the twelfth and thirteenth centuries.

The question set by Archbishop Temple, 'Whether the Bible is supposed to be itself the revelation, or to be the record of the revelation' has had a great impact on modern theological discussion. To say as Temple did that 'the traditional doctrine has rather been that the Book itself is the revelation',[3] seemed to Father Kelly a simplification of the witness of tradition. But in his own reflections on the Old Testament Father Kelly had a way of going directly to the event, without even noticing the interpretation given by the prophet or the prophetic historian. Archbishop Temple wrote that 'the principle of revelation is the coincidence of event and appreciation',[4] admitting that appreciation might come long after the event. Father Kelly sometimes seemed to be appreciating the event for the first time. An example is his admiration for Jael: 'a fierce Bedawin woman with the pluck of a battalion and nerves of steel, seeing the enemy of her God on the run, makes up her mind . . . to get in somewhere and to get in effectively, even if it was only with a tent peg.'[5] This is not,

[1] In a lecture on the eighteenth century.
[2] In a letter to Professor Dorothy Emmet, quoted by her in her chapter on Temple's philosophy in F. A. Iremonger, *William Temple*, Oxford, 1948, pp. 532–3.   [3] *In Nature, Man and God*, pp. 307–8.   [4] Ibid., p. 315.
[5] *SSM Quarterly*, vol. 13, no. 52, Christmas 1914, p. 110.

I believe, a paraphrase of 'Blessed above all women shall Jael the wife of Heber the Kenite be', but an appreciation of the event as seen. So Father Kelly saw, not only what the Bible sees, but the signs of the times in the history of the Church, and where he could, in the world of his own day. History to him was more than the record of events, but it was also very much more significant than any theory. 'Theories', he would say, 'are the theories of theorists.' People of average intelligence and moderate ability, if they think, are more likely to see what is really happening.

The battle of Father Kelly's life was for theological reformation. He wrote in 1906:[1] 'The religious reformation for which we are all hoping must, like all real and permanent religious movements, be founded upon a new theological principle; . . . new only in the sense in which the teaching or thought or ideas of Cyprian, Origen, Augustine, Athanasius or Cyril were new, in which life is always new, growing from the latent seed of the one Sower, having waited for the spring.' He had defined this earlier when he wrote: 'the real and central hinge of any hope of a religious regeneration . . . lies in substituting faith as the dominant religious motive instead of feeling, the delight of learning, beholding, enjoying, obeying . . . for the mere enjoyment and possession of a comfortable sentiment within one's own individuality.' In other words religion must be controlled by theology.

Just as this began to be more than an aspiration, and in some sense a solid reality transforming the whole fabric of modern religion, first in Europe and then in Britain, Father Kelly himself was slowly retiring more and more completely into his own room. His last engagement outside Kelham was a retreat for secretaries of the Student Christian Movement in July 1938. He knew enough of what was happening after

[1] *Ad fratres*, privately circulated to the brethren.

35

that to have some exciting correspondence from time to time
with Miss Dorothy Sayers. Two or three times T. S. Eliot
sat by his fire and tried to make him hear. But by then he
really was 'the old man', infirm, at times querulous, a legend
and a principle, but an uncomfortable principle in a variety
of senses, himself distrustful of recent developments in the
Church of England and in the Anglo-Catholic movement,
and therefore in his own Society's liturgical and theological
life, and therefore himself regarded by many of the younger
brethren as a drag on movement. While he knew and approved
the revival of theological interests in England and on the
continent, he could no more agree with the Anglo-Catholic
arguments against the scheme of Church union in South India
than he could with the scheme itself. The difficulty may be
briefly stated in this way, that while Anglo-Catholics com-
plained of the acceptance of episcopacy without a theory of
its nature and meaning, he found that the scheme implied in
more than one place that the historic episcopate was a practical
expedient, and not a mystery transcending human understanding. If accepting episcopacy without a theory meant
accepting a transcendent mystery, he approved. In the same
way at an earlier stage he could not approve the Anglo-
Catholic arguments against the Prayer Book of 1927, although
he had his own criticisms.

On both these issues he was more discerning than many in
the younger generation, and on the question of South India
he had sufficient support within his own Society to secure at
least a certain measure of detachment from the Anglo-
Catholic campaign against schemes of reunion. Dr Visser 't
Hooft said about him (in 1932) that he 'comes perhaps nearer
to combining in his life and teaching all that is best in Catholi-
cism and Protestantism than any other Christian alive.'[1] This

[1] *Anglo-Catholicism and Orthodoxy*, London, 1933, p. 174.

was in comment upon a passage in *Catholicity* (1932): 'I think what St Paul said of human religions is equally true of our schisms: "The times of this ignorance God winked at, but now commands all men everywhere to repent." . . . I do not think men are ever wholly wrong, except in thinking they are wholly right.'[1]

This was Father Kelly's prophetic word to his time. In another mouth it might have been commonplace, but no one could ever suspect him of not caring intensely about theological truth. His habit and his way of life delivered him from the suspicion of vagueness and woolliness that beset Maurice (not perhaps without some justification). No one ever suspected him of being anything but a theologian, even when he said the most alarming things. No one could deny or even question the faith that lay behind his continual outbursts of scepticism: 'Do we know anything?' Therefore he was uniquely fitted to find a way for the Ecumenical Movement from the liberal to the theological phase. His part in that should secure him a place, not only in the history of the Church of England, but in the world history of the Catholic Church.

Father Alfred, his younger brother, a man of extraordinary physical vigour, who played tennis for the Kelham first six when he was over seventy, died after a short illness on 19th March 1950. He was twelve years younger, and his unexpected death came to Father Kelly as a direct summons. By that time he had been confined to his room altogether for more than a year. Most of the day however he still sat up in bed with a blanket over his shoulders and his board in front of him, reading and writing notes on innumerable scraps of paper, generally of the kind that had been intended for wrapping margarine. He took a certain interest in the prospects of

[1] P. 84. *Catholicity*, like *The Gospel of God*, was published by the SCM Press.

a 'diamond jubilee' for the first beginnings in Vassall Road. As late as September he was at work on the article already cited on what he called 'the Mousehole',[1] but at the end of the month what was left of his physical strength began to fail. Mercifully his last illness was very brief. He 'went home', to use his own expression, on October 31st, the eve of All Saints, 1950, three months after his ninetieth birthday.

[1] *SSM Quarterly Paper*, vol. 51, no. 177, December 1950 (posthumous).

THE GOSPEL OF GOD

PREFACE

THIS book is concerned with the most common-place subject possible, which has been called the Riddle of Life, and by some people the Riddle of the Sphinx. Is there any meaning or purpose for life? How can we find or follow it? It is the essence of a riddle that so many possible or apparent answers suggest themselves, and they do not fit it. It is the essence of a good riddle that the answer is quite simple, and overlooked partly because it is so simple.

It is obvious that this riddle is no mere game, nor a problem of intellectual curiosity. It is a desperately serious question for us all. To a large extent, we all have to shape our lives according to what we can see to be worth doing.

The subject of this book is common-place, and the treatment is as common-place as I can make it. I am not dealing with philosophic or scientific questions, but with the questions everybody feels, and in the way the common-place everybody feels them. Philosophers and scientists have thought more and know more of our difficulties than we do, and I have made use of their work so far as they help us to understand ourselves better. The book began from an address to students at Swanwick, and I have tried to work it out in two Parts.

We start from the quite obvious moral necessity of finding a life-purpose, but our life is beset with contradictions, which we must face. When we try to evade them, we only make confusions. This part of the book has been extraordinarily difficult to write. All these baffling perplexities of ours form a single whole complex. I might have made a list of questions and dealt with them one at a time. I do not think that would

have been of any use at all. They are not intellectual difficulties which can be disposed of by careful explanations; they
are life difficulties which are never really disposed of at all.
It is impossible to avoid repetitions, just because at each point
the whole mass rushes up again.

This first part is negative and unsatisfying; for the true
values of life cannot be found in us, nor in any ideals of ours.
As we examine them, it becomes increasingly evident that
they lie in God; they are given in a Gospel of what God has
done (Chap. VII). The questions of life are always being
re-stated; the difficulties are always much the same. The
orthodox creeds provide the only answer to them I ever
heard of.

I had intended, and made some attempt, to show what this
Gospel amounted to in actual life, but the book is already
sufficiently long. If I am to talk also of the Christian life, of
the difference which 'faith in God' makes to us morally and
religiously—socially, in regard to our relations with others;
personally, in regard to our own relations with God, in prayer,
worship, perhaps the use of the Bible—I think that must wait
for another time—if God wills, and God's children want it.

To the common-place difficulties of life, therefore, I believe the answer lies with an equally common-place orthodoxy.
I think people do not understand orthodoxy, because they
have not really understood their difficulties. Just as I might
have simplified the book if I could have treated the difficulties
as merely intellectual, so I might have simplified it by putting
the orthodoxy first, and then showing how it met the difficulties of life. I do not do it, because I never have done it.
I doubt if anybody's life is really made that way. When I was
young, I learnt to believe the simple Evangelical and Bible
faith current in middle Victorian times. It answered all the
difficulties I knew of. I have never to my knowledge seriously

doubted it, nor changed it. That Gospel was to me a single whole thing of infinite significance; it was not a list of doctrines, severally numbered. Since I began to think, I have dabbled in a whole host of things—science, philosophy, psychology, history, Biblical criticism, to say nothing of law, economics, and many more. I never had either the brains or the scholarship to be an authority on any of them. Being an entirely common-place person—as will hereinafter no doubt sufficiently appear—I tried to learn all I could that would help me to understand the life common to us all. No doubt my ideas developed a great deal. I boggled at Darwinism a long time, though the monkeys never troubled me (Mendelism, when I heard of it, was a great joy). Once I definitely tried to reject Biblical criticism; nor, at first, did the significance of sacramentalism and of the Church appeal to me. Nevertheless, as I gained any new vision of the infinite content of life, I always found the Gospel—and I may add, the Bible—there before me, shedding its own light thereon, but still beyond and above. I found a meaning for things I had seen and read twenty times, but which I had been too ignorant to notice. I never supposed that I should find a Gospel *in* science, philosophy, or history, but I was quite sure that the Gospel of life would be a Gospel *to* all these.

So far as I can remember, I never had the least notion of 'defending' my faith, nor have I in this book. I wanted it to defend me against all sorts of temptations, perplexities, horriblenesses. But 'orthodoxy' was never to me a presupposition, or premise, from which answers were deduced. All the questions here discussed I worked at for years, found hints of answers and followed them up. As in modern physics, hints gained in one quarter illuminated the perplexities, or joined on to hints, somewhere else. To me they are tools for use. I can seldom remember where I learnt them. I learnt almost everything first from Maurice; then I learnt it over again—several times.

'Orthodoxy', word or idea, meant to me at first very little. Afterwards it came to mean a great deal. I believe in One universal, that is, catholic, Spirit of God. When a multitude of good Christian people have found the joy of life in something, I was pretty sure they had found something. I am not talking of their 'opinions'. Possibly they did not always understand themselves nor the point at issue; also possibly, I did not understand them. That not uncommon anxiety to explain that one's beliefs are, of course, quite different from what people ever believed before seems to me a little more superstitious than its opposite. If any one cannot see what the Creeds have got to do with his life, it is only honest to say so. But if I cannot understand what scientists are trying to tell me, e.g., about the structure of the atom, I should think myself a fool if I said, 'It is no use', though evidently it is no use to me till I can understand it. I wait and go on trying.

I ought to say something as to the three classes of readers specially contemplated. I do not want to bore readers with an autobiography of no special interest, but the question is largely personal.

1. As to scholars, philosophic or other. By the necessities of my work for nearly forty years, I have read much more scholars' work than most merely average people have time for. Although I have no claims to attention on the ground of scholarship, I should like to think that even real scholars might find an interest in seeing what the merely average mind does make of their work.

Passing over the scholars, therefore, the difficulties of life affect different people in two ways:

2. Simple and practical people are apt to despair of any

understanding of Life, and they are the people who lie nearest to my heart. But I am a singularly incapable person myself, and I am not very confident of my power to help them, though I am always thinking of them.

3. Though I am neither a scholar, nor a practical person, I am, within my own limits, a thinker and an idealist. I address myself, therefore, primarily to my kind, and am mainly concerned with the difficulties and confusions which beset idealism and idealists. It is for us to help common and practical people. I am sure many of us are helping much more effectively than I ever do. At the same time, the present perplexed state of affairs, the divisions among idealists, and the disastrous split between idealists and common people, might suggest a little doubt whether we have got our message quite straight.

In result, this book is a reconsideration of ideals, and it is addressed to all three classes.

Concerning style, I have written with a certain familiarity, as a soul speaking to souls. I have referred to the intellectual, scientific or philosophic, aspects or theories, not for their own sakes, but for the help they could give us, and because of the difficulties which, to some, they create.

Familiarity degenerates into colloquialism and slang, which a good many people not unreasonably dislike. On the other hand, there is no subject—unless it be modern psychology—which suffers so much from unreal phraseology as 'religion', and it does seem to me vitally important that we should realize exactly what we are saying and doing in the simplest terms.

Aquinas (after Aristotle) distinguishes good *secundum rem* ('real' good) from good *secundum rationem* (as we estimate it), i.e., the desirable. It is a very important distinction, but it comes home much more simply if you call them Good and Nice. To the child mother is always 'good', but mother, on occasion, can be 'simply horrid'.

This I was asked to explain: There are certain nouns—religion, piety, morality, tradition, modernity; there are certain theories as to their use and nature, which may be called religionism, pietism, moralism, traditionalism, or modernism; there are adjectives, applicable to the ideas or people concerned—religionist, pietist, moralist, traditionalist, modernist. When the theories are popular, the adjective is claimed with pride; where they are unpopular, the adjectives are regarded as offensive or derogatory. To my mind, they are simply descriptive.

We all love doing things, I call it 'love of bragging', and that too is descriptive. If we are that way, why not recognize it? Is it sarcasm? Seeing how easily we can deceive ourselves, if we or our ideas cannot stand a bit of rough statement, it is just as well to suspect that we, or they, are trying to cover something up.

I quite recognize that a conventional colloquialism is as conventional as any other form of rhetoric, and I can only warn readers solemnly that the worth of any idea is its truth; that a thing is no more true because the way of saying it sounds smart and clever, than because it sounds solemn and profound. My readers can reach to truth only by the gift of God, with the effort and sincerity of their own souls. It is never an easy thing, and I do not suppose the book is easy, but the difficulties are not necessarily of my making. So far as I know myself, I have simply tried to be helpful. If colloquialism, homeliness, even a bit of sarcasm, helped to clear things up, as also if rhetoric of other kinds would help, I used them, consciously and deliberately; if not, I cut them out. If some people find the style irritating, there was a Saloon

Notice out West: 'Gentlemen are requested not to shoot at the organist. He is doing his best.'

I have to thank two dear friends for many drastic criticisms, which have led to much re-writing; otherwise this would have been an even poorer book than, perhaps, it is. They tell me, however, that the book is wanted now, and now it must go in.

Whatever defects the book may have, there is a very simple argument running through it, which I will add to the Table of Contents, by which everybody may know in each chapter where he has got to.

HERBERT KELLY, SSM

Kelham, Newark-on-Trent,
6th July, 1928

NOTE TO SECOND EDITION

In preparing a second edition, I have space only to reply to a friend who criticized this book as 'pessimistic'. I should not like to admit it was. There are a great many pessimisms in life. I dragged them into the foreground, deliberately, defiantly, joyously, with intent to show how the glory of Christ has transfigured them into a triumphant optimism.

Someone else, replying to the critic, said, 'Do tell people to read the last two chapters first.' That is good sense. So many of us are only annoyed at hearing about our futilities until we know how they have been met, and what God means by them. But then there are others on whom the Gospel story gets no grip, because they have never realized the difficulties it meets.

So I would say – if you do not feel any difficulty in life, you had better take the book as it stands, begin with its unbeliefs, and go on

47

to its faith. You will know then what faith means. If these unbeliefs are already too near you, and too pressing, begin with the faith. Then you will find it worth while to see how the unbeliefs, for all their seriousness, are something one can laugh over.

H.K.

THE CHALLENGE OF LIFE

I AM trying to write a book about God, and the place God has in our life. In the common way of talking what is concerned with God is called Religion. It will naturally be assumed that I am writing about religion, a subject on which people are always writing books. Some of us think it a very important subject, while others deny its importance. I only want to insist that God and Religion are not quite the same, although in a book about God one cannot very well help talking about religion.

Religion properly denotes all the human activity, sometimes the practices—what man does—sometimes his feelings, sometimes his ideas or thoughts, so far as they are concerned with God. We generally use the word in its specific sense of things like church-going, prayer, or meditation, which are directly concerned with God, but anything may come into it that is done as for God's sake. In all cases, however, religion is some activity of our own.

The New Testament very seldom uses the word at all. St Paul speaks of religion twice, and twice he uses an equivalent word we might translate as 'cult', but only when speaking of heathenism or of pharisaic Judaism, never of Christianity. St James speaks of 'pure religion' as consisting in visiting the afflicted and in moral purity, without referring to its specific sense.

Religion is, by origin, a heathen word. The heathen were always talking about it, while they had very vague and uncertain ideas about God. Christianity, on the other hand, is first of all and distinctively a Gospel, a very wonderful story or message about God, about what God has done. Thence, it is a Faith, and this word means, not an acceptance of certain doctrines or beliefs, but a trust in God, and in what God has worked or effected in the way related in the story. The New Testament writers habitually speak of Christianity as a message or as a faith.

Of course, it is true that there is also a Christian religion. If we believe the Gospel, then there is a practice, a feeling, a thinking, which make up our response to that faith, but it is the peculiarity of Christianity that the religion is and remains secondary; the faith is primary. The order makes a great difference. I think it is plain, and it is most important that we should realize, that to believe in God, to look to and think about God and what God does is not the same as believing in religion, which in fact means believing in and thinking about certain practices and states of mind of our own.

In any case it is my business here to talk about what God means to us, what God means in a world, what difference faith in God would make in our lives; to show how men have tried to believe in God, how some at least have been brought to believe in God; to show how men can lose that faith, why faith is so difficult to hold even when we have reached it. As I shall try to explain, I think, so far as we today are concerned, the confusion in our minds between God and that state of our own which we call Religion is a very large part of our difficulties. Indeed, I cannot help thinking that, certainly with many people, the worship of 'Religion' has become a great stumbling-block in the way of the worship of God.

This way of talking about religion may seem strange. Whether there is any reason for it we shall see presently; anyhow if I am to talk about God, I at least ought not to start with religion, but still less ought I to start by talking of morality. If religion is our response, our way of holding ourselves towards God, morality is concerned with our conduct towards men, ourselves or others. But then I am not talking of God only as a thing apart, but of God, and his world. Our Gospel is a story about God, but it is a Gospel preached to men; it is a Gospel for human life. I shall have a good deal to say in the next chapter about the complexities and contradictions of human life, which a gospel may perhaps unravel and which certainly want unravelling, but I will not start with difficulties and contradictions. I will start with something which at least seems to be quite simple and easy to follow.

What is the difference between a really fine chap, a decent chap, and a rotter? What makes them so different? Quite simply, as I imagine it, a fine chap is one who has found a purpose worth living for, or worth dying for. The higher that purpose is, and the more wholly he gives himself to it, the finer man he will be. In the war, lots of rotters became fine chaps—at least 'for the period'—since war like sport has this characteristic—that at least for a time it sets before you a single, common aim, clear, unquestionable, and absorbing. A decent chap is one who has got near enough to a purpose to know there is such a thing. The purpose may not be high enough, or perhaps the vision is not clear enough, greatly to exalt his life, yet there is enough at least to keep his life straight. A rotter is a person who has no purpose in life except pleasure-grubbing. A primitive savage digging with a bit of stick for grubs and roots is only a picture of a highly civilized you or me digging with a bit of money for a 'good time', which is a desperately poor way of living. If you can find a purpose in life, following it you will get a lot of hard work, together with some other things which our Lord called 'persecutions'; incidentally, you will also get exhilaration, joy, fun, in bucketsful. If you seek this excitement and fun in themselves, you will never get more anyhow than spoonsful. This is called 'enjoying oneself', and the self is not worth enjoying. So is life made that all real joy begins from forgetting the self for something better worth going after.

It is my purpose to show what difficulties there are in giving oneself to a purpose; how men have tried to get round those difficulties; where the true purposes of life really lie, and how they come to us, and how we can, in turn, follow them.

THE PARADOX OF HUMAN LIFE:
ITS DIFFICULTIES & CONTRADICTIONS

I MAKE my start, then, from a simple moral principle that no life is worth living, and no life is really enjoyable, except by virtue of its purpose. It is not a very original observation. It is the commonest of all moralizings. It rests upon a belief that human life has a real, I might say an infinite, value, and purpose is the pursuit of that value. The needless death of a child pains us, because those values seem to have been missed. It seems to us even more sad when the real values of life are thrown away for the sake of mere pleasure. If we watch, those who follow this moral principle least and those who scoff at it most betray no small consciousness of its truth. The feverish restlessness of pleasure-grubbing is evidently an attempt to fill up a vacancy somehow. The bitterness of the scoffer is evidence of his disappointment; partly, of his jealousy at those who found what he has failed to find; often no doubt of his dread that he might find something to disturb his easy-goingness.

Such people make us rather impatient, and we may overlook the very real difficulties they find. In the first place what do we mean by a purpose? Money-making, even pleasure-grubbing, are purposes, though they seem purely selfish. On the other hand, the whole progress of history seems to turn on the achievements of men who heard the call of great ideals, and their memory inspires us. This is what I mean by idealism. Those of us who believe in ideals, think of them, and want to give ourselves to them, we call idealists. I am one myself.

In this chapter I am talking specially to them, but we idealists represent rather a special class. There are a good many other people to be considered.

First, much the larger part of mankind are quite simple-minded. They are content to do simple and obvious duties in a simple and obvious way. We may call that an ideal of life, but they do not call it anything. When we idealists get talking of high ideals, I think we are apt to forget how many people there are who cannot even understand what we are driving at, although they are not in the least necessarily 'rotters'.

The other day I went into the workshop to get some sort of edge on my big axe. I got someone to help with the emery-wheel. Our professional carpenter, who was working there, made some caustic remarks about 'steel temper', and drove us over to the grindstone, which we watered profusely and prepared to start. The sight of us was too much for the carpenter. He lounged over, took the axe out of my hand, worked the stone himself, and in five minutes put an edge on that axe, such as little amateurs are allowed to dream of on Sundays, if they've been good. I never asked that carpenter what his ideals in life were. I doubt if he would have known what I was talking about, and I do not think the answer would have been helpful in an ethical book, but he and I are friends, so to speak; also he is a very good carpenter.

I have more ideals than you need listen to just now. A really sharp axe is one of them, but I cannot sharpen an axe and he can. If you can remember this story, I think it may be found to illustrate a good many things.

Secondly, there is a class of people who call themselves 'practical', and who definitely dislike our idealism. Their attitude may be given in a quite common saying: 'It would be very nice if the world and mankind were different from what they are, but we have to deal with things as we find them, not as we should like them to be or as we dream of them.' That attitude rather annoys us, because it is so definitely opposed to our own. It seems to provide a shelter for the merely selfish conservatism of the well-satisfied. But many of these anti-idealists are extraordinarily good people with a very high sense of duty. It seems to me in plain fact that the ideal and practical characters belong to two different callings. Difficult as it is, we must not only put up with one another; we must contrive to learn from one another. The distinction will pursue us all through this book, and, if I seem to be writing mostly as an idealist to idealists, the practical and the simple-minded are never out of my mind. I should like to think that some of them will read this book, and feel that I have understood them.

Lastly, there is the very pathetic class of those who have tried and failed. There is a large crowd on our beach, loitering and chatting, occasionally looking at the water and dabbling in it, many of whom have never thought of making for the pier diving-board. But among them, there is a far larger number than we think who at least waded in valiantly when they were young, with ambitions as high as any of us, but who scrambled back in perplexity when they found how different the sea was from a swimming-bath.

The mere existence of these classes is enough to prove that the pursuit of a life-purpose involves some very serious difficulties; the higher the purpose is set the greater the difficulties will be. About these difficulties, I want to begin with two warnings.

My first warning is this, that the real difficulties of our life are themselves very difficult to see, to describe, or even to explain. When one talks of the difficulty of high ideals, one thinks of all the obvious difficulties of devising means, overcoming opposition, and so forth, but these—which I might call 'the soldiers' difficulties'—are the least part. I am talking of paradoxes, and a paradox is something which seems obviously false, even absurd, yet is vitally true. Life is full of contradictions, that is, of principles which are apparently opposed, yet both true, even indispensable, and that, of course, is a paradox. As this chapter is mainly occupied with the contradictions of life, I will not give instances now. I only urge that, however annoying they may be, we must face them.

My second warning is that we idealists are peculiarly unwilling to face our difficulties, and that is not good for us. We are at heart enthusiasts. We have an intense *a priori* conviction, faith, vision, intuition of the value of life-issues. These uncomfortably practical people are *a posteriori* folk, and they appeal to facts. No doubt we also can quote some facts, which they perhaps ignore, as we perhaps ignore theirs. In truth, it annoys us to have the very inspiration of our life criticized and analysed, but being annoyed at things does not take them away. It only means that we shall run into them in the dark when we are not prepared. That is where failures begin.

It is not, then, because I do not believe in idealism, but because I do, that, having given in Chapter I my profession of faith as an idealist, I am going in this chapter to state the case of our practical friends. It is just here, maybe, that we need to learn from them. They say, 'the facts, the actual experience, of life does not bear out our idealism.' I believe that they are in the main right. If we are to justify our faith —as I am sure it can be justified—we shall have to look a good deal beyond human purposes and experience; for, as I shall show in the next chapters, men have always believed that this life did not really explain itself.

I shall put my points in rather brutal, even vulgar, language. I do not want to hurt people's feelings, but it is all too easy for us to cover up awkwardnesses by well-sounding phrases, which only prevent our realizing exactly what we have said.

I *The Paradox of Self-importance*

It may be a little easier if I divide these chapters into sections, as far as I can, and this section may deal with a single idea. 'A paradox is something obviously false, which is nevertheless true.' Is not self-importance somewhat paradoxical? We think it a hateful thing. I quite agree, yet in fact, we are all working on it. It is just one of these things which we do not like to recognize.

I said that we draw a great deal of our inspiration from the history of certain heroes and their achievements. That is a very old fashion. We have all heard of Smiles and Lubbock, and the great examples of success they held up for our imitation. They were always being thrown at us, and they already bored us, when I was a boy. There is a magnificent poem beginning:

> Lives of great men all remind us
> > We can make our lives sublime,
> And departing leave behind us
> > Footprints on the sands of time.

I think these lines express our ideal sufficiently well, but to whom do they apply? I once had a friend who was really clever. He thought the clergy ought to be all 'leaders of thought'. I suggested to him that 16,000 leaders of thought (exclusively Anglican) would be rather distracting. If we take to leaving footprints on that scale, the sands of time would be trodden down flat, and there would be no footprints at all. I think we forget that greatness and smallness, cleverness and stupidity, are comparative terms. If we were all five times as clever as we are, there would be just as many clever leaders and just as many comparatively stupid people as there were before. After all, average people make up the bigger part of the world, and do the bigger part of its work.

The words cannot apply, and mostly they do not appeal, to the general mass of common and simple people. There are a good many of us who would say that lives of great men chiefly remind us what very small people we are. No doubt great people with great abilities or other advantages may do great things, but we pretty well know we can't. The big ventures are outside our reach or understanding. It might be rather nice to feel ourselves sublime, but we do know we can make ourselves fairly comfortable. It is not an ambitious, nor a high, ideal but, if pressed, we are inclined to make the most of it. It is all we are likely to reach.

Certainly, however, a great many of us are ambitious, especially when we are young. We may not be very clever; it is rather odd how little ability affects ambition. We want to do something, something creative—'constructive' is a favourite word—something big enough to be worth doing. Merely 'wanting' is poor stuff, and comes to nothing. We *mean* to do this something, though we hardly know what it is, or is going to be. When I was young, I always meant to set the Thames on fire. When I went to Japan, I was over fifty, and I was quite sure Tokio Bay could be set on fire if one studied it carefully enough, and I meant to do it. I am quite impenitent. When I am asked to speak at Swanwick or to preach somewhere, or if I write this book, it is with the full intention of making a conflagration as big as Latimer's 'candle'—which you will remember in English history. Platforms, pulpits, and printers' paper are just kindling. Why else should one take all this trouble?

Very well, in effect I have said—I mean to be a great person. I might have said—I mean to be sublime, but some-

58

how I shrink from that. To you, I have no doubt, both seem equally foolish. So they do to me. We have left off reading Longfellow, not merely because his ideal of greatness is too difficult of attainment, but much more because it reminds us too openly of our own self-importance. We talk rather solemnly of self-development and self-fulfilment, yet they are only fine names for bragging. We use the solemn words because we do not like to recognize what a large part this joy of bragging takes in our lives. 'Victory!'—the very sound of the word is as appealing as the substance. And there are victories of many kinds. You may overcome 'things'. That is the joy of the doctor, farmer, and engineer, of the scientific discoverer, the explorer, and rock-climber. It is often most acute when you get a living opponent—as in cricket. With every ball he can hit, the batsman exults against the bowler, who sticks doggedly to the conviction that he will have the last brag yet. This is the instinct of controversial politics. 'I demand my rights'—or somebody else's rights. It does not much matter which so long as one can get up a good scrap with the people round. If the other people concede the demand, dignity requires we should accept the concession, but at heart we are a little disappointed; for there has been no victory. We do not really want the aforesaid rights half as much as we want to knock the other man down and take them off him. In theological controversies notably, there is very little satisfaction in being 'right', unless you can show that the other man is wrong. In theology, as in parliament, it is very difficult to get people interested in a non-controversial subject.

Perhaps we are not all so combatant. It always puzzles me to notice among the mountains how many people prefer walking up a path, and apparently never realize that the precipice is much better fun, just because it is more difficult.

Even they, however, enjoy overcoming distance, and that also is a personal success. I will not instance the so-called 'selfish greed' of business. The ordinary parish parson, one of the simplest minded, and, in his way, one of the most heroic and self-less class of men I know, labours for his own parish, preaches his own ideas or convictions just as I write this book, in the intent to succeed, and, if I suceed, it will be *my* success, just as the batsman makes *his* score, and the business man *his* pile. We are sorrowfully aware of 'mixed motives'. How can we get them unmixed? My ideas are mine, and my motives are mine. What else can they be? And if I am right in saying that all true joy in life comes from forgetting oneself, all this self-assertion hardly seems the best way of attaining self-forgetfulness.

Let us see where we have got to. There is no true life without purpose even though the great multitude of simple people never attempt to formulate their ideals. When we do try to formulate our own, the more worthy we try to make them, is there not something absurd when we see how largely our courage is moulded out of self-importance, and is in the end moulded *into* self-importance. It is at this that the practical people scoff.

II *Ideals and the Experience of Life*

So far I have been talking about a common principle involved in the very start. Now we will take our second section, and look at what actually becomes of our great purposes. I am afraid the results are very often of a kind too grim to be thought of as absurd.

(1) *The Confusion of Ideals.* There are quite a number of us idealists who are sure we could set the world straight if only those stupid 'other people' would listen to us. Unfortunately, they are so very stupid that instead of listening,

they think exactly the same of their ideas. In this country, politically we generally keep two, or maybe three sets of people who are quite sure they can set everything right. Now and then we have a General Election to decide which set shall be allowed to try. I can remember people lamenting our lack of great leaders. I am not sure about the greatness, but it might be argued that there were too many, anyhow so many that no one can make up his mind which to follow.

If we look further afield, matters are much more serious. Is it not a plain fact that the world is being torn in pieces by idealists more than by any other set of people one can name? And I will not talk of theological parties. We like to say that the Great War was caused by greed, violence, and 'nationalism', but at least to a very large extent it was a war of ideals, which is the true meaning of *Kultur*. Everywhere we are troubled by a condition we call unrest, which, in fact, means an unsatisfied idealism.

(2) *The Strife of Parties*. These ideals begin, seem to begin, are counted as beginning, with great personalities. At least I suppose so; for, in spite of all our modern worship of personalities, few things are so hard as to make sure how far great men originate a movement, how far they only pick up, perhaps formulate, what others are already thinking, perhaps only give it a name. Certain it is, however, that a movement is constituted, not by great people, but by the multitude of little people who join up, and make a team.

Now, when I talked of setting the Thames on fire, it sounded absurd. It was even offensive, because I said *me*, and whatever one hopes, feels, or means, one is not expected to talk that way of oneself. I do not know if we little people are really modest, but most of us are timid, and timidity is a useful substitute for modesty. We like to coagulate in parties, groups, associations, where the shrinking *me* can take shelter behind the pretentious majesty of *us*—which does not need to be modest at all, and certainly, for the most part, isn't.

It is, I think, evident that these unexpected difficulties and absurdities arise from a contradiction too little observed. When we think of the great purposes of life in which we would take a part, they are not only great, they are infinite (the Latin word is *immensus*—immeasurable) and eternal. If, however, these purposes are to become ours, or 'mine', they have to become purposes of a self, to be brought within the measure of a self.

Let us take Luther, Calvin, Loyola, as three really great men who lived close together, influenced one another very much, and exercise today an immense influence on all our lives. How terribly certain they were of themselves, not only of the rightness and truth, but of the all-sufficiency of the ideas they had taken up. It is, in the first place, just their self-confidence, secondly, the apparent completeness with which their ideals became formulated, which made their influence so powerful. If you chose to be a Lutheran, a Calvinist, or an Ultramontane, you would know exactly what you had to say about everything, and there would be nothing to doubt.

But I do not think we do these men justice. They hardly do themselves justice. It is true they shout at you, show no obvious sense of having anything to learn, or that others may have something worth saying of a different kind, yet there is in all of them some consciousness of the infinity of things, of the complexity at least of their own ideals.

On the other hand, that collective self we call a 'party' cannot even imagine anything more complicated than a programme. As it becomes organized to make a movement, quite generally under the direction of some unseen group of men whom no one would call great, whose very names and manipulations are unknown, its mind is narrower and harder, its policy often more violent and cruel, than anything possible to a merely individual self. There is a caution and hesitancy in Darwin, which is not always evident in the dogmatism of late Victorian Darwinism. Kant's idealism is the groundwork of the German idea of *Kultur*. Rousseau is the initiator of the French Revolution, as Karl Marx of Bolshevism. Would any of them have recognized the use made of their ideals? Perhaps Marx would. I do not know.

(3) *Disillusion*. So far for our idealizing, whether we be great people who initiate ideals, or small people who only join up. If the world asks us what becomes of ideals, we cannot deny that, if they have led to some, perhaps to much, good, it has been at the cost of terrible evil. It is not always easy to say which was greatest. But then these great ideals which have stamped their effects on history, are the select few. If you try to count up the number of us who wanted, and even meant, to set the Thames on fire, we shall find it still harder to say that anything in particular came of our ambitions. What are we to make of the bare, ugly facts of disillusion and failure?

Just now disillusion is with us all a very serious fact, indeed, the most serious fact, in European politics. We had a war on, and ideals ran high. Now we were brought to it, we would make an end of that old evil world of suspicion, jealousy, strife; we would set up a new kingdom of reasonableness. Heroism, devotion, life, were all poured out like water. Then came long years of endurance and hope, expectation and disappointment, in which ideals grew sodden in the endless downpour for want of sunshine, till nothing was left except a dogged determination to get through somehow without surrender to the powers of evil. Well, in the end we did win. Won what, except that we staved off another, more terrible, ending?

There is nothing new in all this, except that it happens to be recent. The history of the middle ages is little but a record of tragedies. The crusades are typical. The final significance of the life of St Francis is the tragedy of its failure. The Hildebrandine ideal of the papacy is the most momentous, the life of Savonarola is the most complete, of all tragedies. But these are special cases. I forget how many mediaeval volumes there are in Migne's *Patrologia Latina*—perhaps eighty—and I could not estimate how many writers are represented. Only a few professed historians ever think of reading most of them. Yet they were all men, I suppose, of considerable ability and of importance in their day.

I have lately been looking through certain volumes of bound pamphlets covering the first half of the nineteenth century, a period full of very momentous developments. They are mostly by solemn and impressive people who thought they had something which needed saying—on Church Rates, Church Reform, on Education, the fifth of November, and other thrilling topics. Was it all worth saying? I do not know. Most of the sermons were 'published by request', and some of the pamphlets reached a second edition, yet they are unbelievably dull reading. Their futility is both pathetic and rather frightening; for are we any wiser? We think we know, but so did they. Do we see the significance of what is happening in our day better than they did in theirs? I wonder. It is not that we cannot do anything—we can do a lot—but so little comes of it. Did our immortal poet quite realize what he was saying? Walking on the sands is a heavy business. We leave footprints all right, and the next tide——?

(4) *Futility*. We are very conscious of the importance of our own doings, because the short-time intervals they occupy act like a high-power lens. Just 'this' stands up clear and

sharp, like a moment of consciousness, even its immediate connections are blurred and out of focus. The rest are not in the picture at all. We try to do the same with history, making everything circle round a few names which are easy to remember. Do we quite realize that this limitation of comprehension on our part is, and is doing the work of, the tide, washing out all the sand footprints of the multitude who passed that way? I ask if we are more than children, playing on the beach, building castles in the air, and then building them in the sand. How long is it since the rocks of Scafell, under whose shadow I write these lines, were laid down molten over the bottom of the sea? Seas have changed to continents and continents to seas many times over. It is only as it were last week that a bored Roman sentry on the Hard Knott Camp watched the road running from Ravenglass through Ambleside over High Street to the Great Wall. Now the Camp is a square of stones, barely showing above the turf. Is our life more than a faint dot in the relentless course of history? Are we not in the hand of cosmic force? Call it fate, luck, what you will, what can we do against it? Some of us dream of initiating movements, and many of us think of ourselves as at least adding our weight. The movements are, I suppose, part of history, and they consist of, are constituted by, a number of pretty average people. But certainly, as one watches their course, it does seem as if most of us were being caught up, swept along, by them, rather than joining by deliberate and individual judgment, just as the drops, 'minims', of water which seem to form a tide have lost their individuality in the common mass. Can we really do anything? Marcus Aurelius was quite sure we could do just nothing, except in the becoming management of our own life, for he is the great apostle of character-building. 'The cosmos bears you, and you drop off like a ripe olive.'

Yet Marcus Aurelius held the supreme power of a Roman emperor.

(5) *Death*. At the present day people do not reckon to be afraid of death. Certainly very many are quite indifferent. Our friends on the beach do not talk about the subject, do not like to think of it, but they acquiesce in the inevitable. If we have to die in the first cold snap, as the flies do, at least we get our sugar while we can. I am no more going to argue against this view, than I am going to argue against pessimism. I do not agree with either. What is to be said on both subjects, we will come to in due course, but we are all too much in a hurry to refute people we disagree with when we ought to be understanding and learning from them. Religious teachers from mediaeval times to the end of the seventeenth century were fond of basing their appeal on a future world which they could picture to their convenience, even while they were conscious of its religious ineffectiveness. Bishop Butler and Wesley appealed to it, but the current was setting against them. In our own day, the blatant vulgarity of spiritualist ideas about the next world has acted as a very useful warning to us.

Just now, I am asking about the meaning of this present life and where we can find it. A medical friend of mine, a very devout man, once remarked to me that in his experience religious people were more afraid of death than the irreligious. He thought it showed how little reality their religion had. The idea was new to me, but I did not agree with him. It is worth noting that Marcus Aurelius was quite prepared even for suicide. 'If the room smokes, I leave it.' The significance of his, and of other, indifference to death is just this, that it is only when one thinks of life as worth living, with purposes worth following, that death, as the end of all effort, seems such a mockery.

So many of us have purposes. We build barns to hold the products; I have built a few myself. There are other people of real capacity who know how to fill them, which is a much more important and more difficult business. We take the Lord's parables too straitly, as if they only applied to those other worldly people who do carnal business. But whether our many goods be measurable in cash values, whether they are the accumulations of learning or science, the achievements of art, or the moral services of social uplift, it is all the same. In an hour when we think not, without any question as to how it fits our plans, this night—'and then whose shall those things be?' That is the mystery of Gethsemane. The human nature of Christ shrank from death, because he knew so well the meaning of life. Birth is a mere potentiality. The life it gives may, always does in the end, flicker out like a candle, whether by a sudden draught or by mere consequence of burning. Death is the natural sacrament of the futility of life, the antithesis, not of birth, but of baptism which is the divine sacrament of the eternal value of life.

We have done now with my two main sections—concerned with a certain root difficulty we find in ourselves, and with the difficulties which the experience of life brings. I have said somewhere that all human life is a dualism, a contradiction, a paradox—of two elements, each true, yet utterly opposed and inconsistent. There is in the end but one dualism, though it meets us in a hundred forms. You may find its contradictions by rows in philosophy or science. Here are some of them:

(a) What we care for is the reality of things, but what experience gives us are appearances, from which we must reason as we best can.

(b) We believe in truth, but what we actually have are notions, opinions, as to what is true.

67

(*c*) Knowledge is concerned with unities. To know a thing is, first, to know it as a whole in the relation of its parts, whether those parts are bits of a machine, or motives in a man's character; secondly, to know its place in the common unity of all things. On the other hand, the basis of all knowledge is a knowledge of differences.

According to our ignorance, the people we group as the scientists or the critics, the scholastics or the reformers, are supposed to be all much the same. So according to our complacency, they are all 'going the same way.' To those who do know, there were over two hundred species of wasps, when last I heard about them. And as knowledge of this kind increases, the enormous multiplication and complexity of differences makes it very difficult to gain a true unity of knowledge under laws which shall be simple, intelligible, and continuous.

These elements of philosophy, of the business of philosophy, underlie all our thinking, but if anyone finds them too abstract to follow, let him only look through the terms, taking them in their common meanings, and I think he will see how they cover or express some of those very obvious difficulties in our life to which I referred above, and which we all know.

'Unity and difference.' Mankind is a unity sharing in a common life, material and mental; oddly enough, that is why we quarrel. We are so much alike, but then we are alike especially in this that we are so very different. We seek unity with one another; we are saddened or irritated at finding that our progress or development is multiplying differences. We know there is unity in truth, but our opinions do not agree. Then we despair of reality; for we can see only what we can see. In the abstract we seek truth and righteousness, but we can only follow what we *think* to be true and good.

Many people are annoyed at these paradoxical statements, but I have been trying to show that it is the facts of life which are paradoxical. The wars of idealisms and the strife of parties are so bitter, because we try to evade paradoxes instead of recognizing them. The opposite mental attitudes of optimism and pessimism, the enthusiasm for ideals and the knowledge of what is practical, reappear in the struggles of freedom and authority, progress and conservatism, very pathetically in the alienation of youth and age.

I have said that there is in the end but one dualism. It appears in the great dissonance of the biological law of evolution. The sparrow thinks of itself, struggles to maintain and to fulfil its own being. Nature thinks only of the propagation and perfection of the species, and, even beyond the species, of the fulfilment of a whole order. The sparrow is not conscious of that dissonance. We are conscious of it, hence the tragedy of our life. And the contradiction as we have it is what I have called 'the illusion of the horizon'. Go where you will, sit in your own room or seek the mountain top, all the world appears as a circle drawn round you as its centre. Life has many compartments—religion and intercourse, politics and science, work and sleep, food and play—but they are all to me parts of my life. It is an illusion, for the world is not made that way; but it is no illusion, it is bare fact, that in that fashion my mind is made. The illusion of the horizon is the illusion of personality.

So, finally, the contradiction of life is summed up thus:

Man—and I am speaking here of the simplest and commonest human soul—is in himself a whole infinite, made for the infinite, yet by himself a small fragment, astray in a vast universe.

Man, infinite in his ideals and purposes, is yet so petty in achievement. Infinite in our aspirations and possibilities, do we not know ourselves in the paltriness of our motives?

Our hope is for the eternal, but our life is very short. We

seek truth and live for good, but our notion of truth and good is limited by self-judgment and self-choice.

And if this is the truth of human life, what real difference is there between the vulgar who have lost hope because they know their own littleness, and the élite who, because they will not confess futility, have found self-complacence?

If we put the question that way, plainly we are once more trying to simplify things by grasping at one side only of a contradiction, since the infinity of man's soul is as true as its littleness. I repeat, I have not been making out a case for pessimism. I am urging the truth of facts which must be faced. I would not have done it, but I know well that the shadow of failure and the threat of disillusion hang over the young almost as much as the fact of them comes upon the old. Even so I would have held my peace, if I did not know that to all questions there is an answer, but it cannot be found by evading the difficulty of facts. That is, indeed, to shirk the greater difficulty of our duties. The answer is not reached but given, and by quite another road.

III

THE VENTURE OF RELIGION:
ITS EXPRESSION OF LIFE

B Y pessimism we mean the theory that evil exists, not merely as an accident of things, but as an irremovable fact, involved in the very fashion of their existence, though we need not be extreme pessimists and maintain that evil is the only, or the most final, fact. But to pick up our points rightly we must be quite clear that the fact—if it is a fact—and the theory that life is so, are not the same. If there is so much evil in life, a pessimistic view did not put it there, even if it can be contended that thinking of the evil makes it worse. A cheery and unseeing optimism, the theory that evil is only an unfortunate accident and can be easily overcome, may be pleasanter for the time being, and may even be wiser if it leads to some sort of remedial action, but it seems not unlikely to lead to disillusion.

Religion, at least as we know it, seems to protest against the pessimistic view, and to offer a way of escape from the fact of evil, but then most of us know very little about religions. Some religions are profoundly pessimistic; so, for instance, was the stoicism of Marcus Aurelius; so is what we call 'Southern' Buddhism (*Hinayana*) of Ceylon and Burma.

I am not going to repeat the warnings I have given above on the subject of religion. I do believe that this effort of human thought and feeling point us to the right road. I do not say that by religion we can reach an optimistic view of life. Is it clear that we ought to? No doubt, religion, with its rich imagination and power of expressing thought and feeling, provides abundant optimisms, just as it can also provide expression for the opposite views. We ought to see life whole, and thereby to see both its good and evil, at least if both are there; see, if it may be, how the two can be reconciled; how man can rise out of evil into good.

There are certain questions, which in studying religion, we need to keep in mind: How does religion face the fact of evil? What hope of victory does it give us? How far can it, considered as a human effort, the noblest, the most hopeful and significant, of human efforts, lead us to that victory?

I have remarked above that most of us know very little about any religions other than our own, and that, I think, is somewhat of a pity, since it leads us into taking all sorts of things for granted, as if they were quite obvious. By considering religions a little more widely and generally, possibly we might understand our own better if only by way of contrast and comparison, though I admit that it is a difficult thing to do. There is no subject in which increased knowledge has shown us such a baffling and confusing multitude of differences. Yet, I believe, there is no subject on which there is so much real unity. There is none, therefore, which shows so well how human limitation breaks up the unity of truth into difference of opinions; why, in consequence, men despair of reaching Reality—as certainly they are particularly liable to do in regard to religion.

I will put first, a single, common position. I maintain that all religions alike, from the most savage to the most cultured and philosophical, begin from, are based upon, one belief or conviction, viz., that that world-force, which is the ultimate basis of an ultimate life and thought, the primary cause, the final end and measure, which disposes of all man proposes, can only be that ultimate intelligence and purpose, which we call the supreme majesty of God.

Professor C. C. J. Webb gives the point far better than I can:

> No conception less than ultimate reality will satisfy the religious consciousness. As knowledge increases and the horizon widens, as the hidden power is dislodged from totem, mountain, wizard, we discover that we have been seeking throughout after nothing less than the Ultimate Reality. The attempt to identify God with the Absolute *is* religion.

Jeremiah puts it still more tersely: 'The gods that have not made the heavens and the earth, shall perish from the earth, and from under the heaven.'

Through what processes men reach this belief, whether it is the conclusion of an obvious reasoning, a result of innate feeling, of direct intuition, of natural instinct; whether it is a mere longing or a pure assumption; what first suggested it, are from some points of view very important questions, but they are very complex questions and very controversial. I should suppose, in fact, that all these processes have been at work; I am never very sure even how far they are different processes and how far they are involved in one another, but if I try to follow out the share each takes, I do not suppose I should convince anybody, and we should distract our minds from the main point.

No doubt, religious belief is, to us and to all men, primarily traditional. We no more invented it separately for ourselves than we invented arithmetic or language. We were taught all these subjects, but none of them is thereby purely traditional. Religion has had in human history an immense, in our own life a very great and complex, development, growing with our growth, changing as we change. We, and mankind at large, have all sorts of motives, have found all sorts of difficulties in accepting the religious conclusion, and have tried all sorts of ways to evade it. Some are intellectual difficulties, yet this religious belief is so little of a mere philosophy that you have to be a very clever philosopher to understand the philosophical objections. I can barely follow them when I have the books before me, and I can never remember exactly what they are without looking them up. There are many quite practical difficulties, only too plain to all of us. Difficulties, developments, evasions have affected our belief, yet the belief persists as something unescapable, natural, inevitable, in some shape or other to the ignorant and to the clever. The most we can do is to ignore it, to say we do not know, to forget it—under a process we call agnosticism, formal or virtual. It is our more immediate business to ask what this belief is and what value it has.

What is this religious belief? I am well aware that many people who know anything of the vast maze of religious forms will repudiate, perhaps rather contemptuously, my oversimple statement of the substance of the religious conclusion. If it is as simple as all that, why is there all this maze of forms? Further, that statement is utterly inapplicable at least to many forms of religion. What has 'the Supreme Majesty of God' to do with the petty spirit-worship we call Animism, which is more akin to magic, and which often ends in devil-worship? What has it to do with Polytheism? It is at least doubtful whether words like intelligence and will can be applied to the philosophic Absolute, 'the totality of Being', or other forms of Pantheism, which lie at the opposite extreme.

I quite realize the force of the objections, but all religions are movements dealing with a central idea—an idea of God. I have summarized the conclusion to which, as I believe, they are all tending. Some religions are of a very primitive kind, and seem to have done hardly more than get started, though, as in child-psychology, it is of interest to see where they do start. There are many roads, and the inconsistent results

74

reached by them lie side by side in men's minds and practices, because they do not know how to reconcile them. Religions are also drawn off, this way or that, by distracting forces.

If I try to give some account of these diversities, it is not for the sake of religious science, nor in order to justify my summary. I believe religion has more to do with the understanding of our life than anything else; therefore, I think it is important we should understand religion, since all the movements at work in these world-religions are at work in us.

Differences in religion, then, come (*a*) from different conceptions men have of a world; (*b*) from different ways or degrees of thinking; (*c*) there are also many evasions in following one's thoughts:

(*a*) *Conceptions of a World*. Everybody, I have suggested, is thinking about the meaning of the world about him, is sure it has a meaning, and is convinced that only intelligence can give a final meaning to anything, only a will can be a final cause. The creative intelligence cannot be ours; for we are only, through many blunders, trying to learn a meaning.

That I call the simple inference, common to everybody, savage or philosopher, however differently they express themselves. The sceptic Hume admitted that the inference was unanswerable.

Voltaire said that the universe was to his reason—like a watch picked up by an ignorant countryman—plainly the result of intelligence and will, even if he did not know what its purpose was. Paley and the orthodox could only repeat his argument.

But, although the thinking is so much alike, there are immense differences in the 'world' about which men think. The Greeks called it the Cosmos, which means an intelligible order'. We apply the word in many senses, though with the

75

same meaning. Sometimes we use it for 'the universe', stars and all; sometimes, for our own planet; sometimes, for the course of human affairs. We also talk of a religious world, a scientific, a musical, a business, and many other worlds, recognizing that each has an 'order' of its own, though each is also a part of a greater world.

The life of the forest-savage leaves no room for big ideas about the world. His mind is taken up with his own personal, very particular and immediate needs, and his religious mind with the 'spirits' of immediate and particular luck. In general he can look after himself if things come out as he plans, but his whole life is lived amongst perils which cannot be anticipated, so that the spirits he thinks most of are evil and dangerous. He once also recognized universal 'gods', but, just because they were good and favourable and therefore did not need cultivating, he first took them for granted, and has now forgotten them.

The civilized man, or city-dweller, lives in several worlds. He is relatively safe so long as his community holds together, but he belongs also to a great natural world in which big or 'universal' ideas—such as, reproduction and growth, the power of the sun and the mystery of the sky—make appeal to him. It is not quite clear what these powers of nature have to do with one another, or with the city. You can make a good many systems—which we call polytheisms—to explain them. But all these large ideas, which have become 'gods', never entirely hide the fact that the individual has also his own concerns, is often badly frightened, and takes refuge in spirit-magic for personal luck, as a good many people do in the twentieth century.

(b) *Different Ways of Thinking*. When I say that all these people were thinking about the world, or worlds, in which they found themselves living, of course, I do not mean that they wrote books or argued things out. They thought, as most of us think, quite unconsciously, vaguely and uncertainly. There were common religious customs, which meant something. There were, or might be, customary explanations, but most people never asked or thought of asking exactly how much the explanations themselves meant. The language was as customary as the practices, yet men did think after a fashion. As generations passed and life changed, so men's ideas changed, they hardly knew how.

But with civilization, security, some leisure, came men we call philosophers; men, that is, who took pains to think definitely, consistently, thoroughly, and to them the old confused, unconscious thinking was intolerable. Though we think, somewhat disjointedly, of many worlds, there is in truth but one world, with one beginning, one law, one cause, however little we can imagine what that Ultimate may be. When thoughtful men realized that, presently everybody became conscious of it; for this thought of the unity of life, the unity of all things, is never far out of our minds, though it is so difficult to come by and so easily forgotten. But when men did come to it, it was not clear that it meant anything. The philosopher might insist, may insist today, on 'the Absolute', or on 'the Totality of Being', as the 'Ultimate of Thought', but to most of us they are all dreadfully abstract words. How does one pray to a Totality of Being? And if the philosopher answered—'You cannot'—what is the use of the phrase? While, therefore, men admitted that 'the god' was one, they went on praying to a multitude of little gods. They do in India today.

(c) *Religious Evasions.* Men's religions are then profoundly affected by their different conceptions of the world, and different ways of thinking. I gave evasion as a third reason for differences. Religion, whatever it comes to, at least begins by thinking of God as a real and effective power of life, but we will deal with that side in the next chapter. When we do, if it is evident why men seek for God, we shall have also to ask why they try to escape from him, to evade the thought of God—why we do for that matter. We must consider also what evasions they and we find.

In this chapter, I have tried to describe what men have done with their religions, but there is one other thing to which I must refer—what religion has done with men, or what it has done for them.

My account of religions is perhaps far too vague and general for scientific purposes, but I am not writing a scientific book. I want to enable people to form some picture of religion as a great effort on the side of man, if not to understand the world and his own life, at least to realize how they might be understood if only one could reach to a God who lies somewhere behind it all. Its very diversities show that that religion is a human effort; since one can trace how all the different factors in men's minds or experiences, as they come into consciousness, affect, shape, modify, the answers men have found, or think they can find. Religion being such, this at least it has done for men—it has provided the deepest and truest expression of all that is in them. It has not done—considered as a human effort, I think it is evident that it cannot do—more than this. It reflects men's noblest aspirations and longings; it reflects, it expresses, also his bewilderment and despair.

At the beginning of this chapter I put three questions as to whether and how far religions help us to face and to escape the evil, and the dread of evil, in our life. I need not repeat the questions, because, thus far at least, it is evident that religion goes with the sciences, philosophies, and other attempts to understand better the nature of the things with which we have to deal. They do, or they may, answer their own questions, but so far as the great questions of life are concerned, so far as we ourselves are concerned, they are only restating the old problems of life in new and much more complex shapes.

There are, however, two respects in which the religious effort is peculiar. In the first place, its notion of a world-problem is far more inclusive. There is nothing in science or philosophy which does not somewhere affect it. But in the second place religion is so inclusive, because, not content with experience, it is trying to reach to something, which, while we believe it is partly revealed in experience, we take to be essentially an Ultimate, existing in himself beyond experience.

This contrast between what is given in experience, and what one infers to exist beyond experience comes out very clearly in a story of Sydney Smith, and it is a point so important that it is worth making clear. Sydney Smith was at dinner with a somewhat blatant sceptic who tried to take a rise out of the parson by expressing manifold doubts about God, religion, Scripture, and other useful topics, but the parson would not be drawn. Towards the end, the sceptic gave it up, and addressing his host thanked him for a very excellent dinner—'And do you doubt the cook?' said the parson.

Nothing could be better, but let us consider exactly what is involved. To the guests the dinner constituted the whole of available experience in the matter. The condition of the foodstuffs taken separately shows unmistakably the scientific results of heat. But the foodstuffs do not appear separately, nor have they been merely heated. The heat and the sequence of dishes have been very carefully adjusted to an artistic and

79

intelligible end, plainly by an artistic intelligence. Sydney Smith boldly said, 'the cook', but the cook was not in the dinner; she was in the kitchen. I have sometimes remarked that if mistresses would remember that the cook was much more than cookery, that she was a woman you might make friends with, it might at times save a lot of trouble. But I know cooks do not always like 'being friends'.

It is the very nature of this attempt to get beyond, to guess at what lies beyond, experience, which involves the difficulty and even the failure of religion; which involves, I would confess, the obvious reason for its absurdities, its superstitions and magic. Science is a plain matter. When you have learnt to understand experience, you will learn how to use it. But how can anyone learn from experience, what is not in experience?

Nevertheless, hopeless as the enquiry may seem to be from the start, does seem to be from its history, men labour at it, cannot let it alone, for reasons equally obvious.

(1) To live without understanding one's life is to live as a rotter; in Scriptural language, it is the life of a fool.

(2) But we can only understand our life, as life in a world, by reference to a whole order of things.

(3) And it is quite plain to us that this order of things is not intelligible just in itself, in the shape in which it presents itself.

(4) It can be understood only by virtue of something beyond itself, which contains the perfection, the completeness, the actuality, of what in the existing world is plainly an incompleteness, a possibility—just as a building, and a half-finished building at that, a mere complex or jumble of timbers and stones, sticking into one another at strange angles, can only be understood by the assumption of builders whose personalities and purposes are being fulfilled in stone and

timber, but are certainly not to be identified with such material substances.

This assumption, this 'faith', is to us a matter of life and death, intellectually and morally. There is neither sense nor decency to be had without it. I call it a matter of 'faith', but it is also good solid reasoning, in regard to our life and the universe, as in regard to buildings and the Voltaire-Paley watch. To treat faith and reason as alternative opposites is shallow and futile, 'a betrayal of the succours which reason offers' (Wisd. 17.12); for faith is the acceptance, the trust, the basing of action, upon what is reasonable, even if our reason is inadequate to its full comprehension. Indeed, no one ever does understand more than a part of that infinite and sacred complex of purpose and motive by which someone builds a cottage that to generations unknown it may be home.

IV

RELIGIOUS REALITY:
EFFECTIVENESS AND VALUE

THE religions men have are in fact, therefore, the expression of their ideas as to an Ultimate Cause or purpose, but the religions are not meant as the expression of ideas. The Ultimate Cause is thought of as Someone actually existent, with whom worship is intended to establish a relation, and who is an object of faith. Faith is a matter so important in religion that both for our own sakes, and for the sake of others, we must try to see exactly what we mean by it, all the more because people use the word in so many different senses; sometimes as the opposite of knowledge, sometimes as the opposite of reason, and in many other ways.

It is simpler to begin with the contrast of knowledge and belief. Setting aside mere loosenesses and the question of degrees of certainty, knowledge belongs in particular to things which we take to be unalterable—such as mathematics, and the great scientific laws—and for whatever can be proved to follow necessarily. The past is always matter of knowledge, because the past is unalterable. I am talking of a distinction in principle. In practice, perhaps some of our scientific laws are not as unalterable as we thought; perhaps also I do not know much of mathematics, nor of what has happened in the past.

In practice, one very often cannot prove things from unalterable laws, but only from bits of evidence which have come one's way. I may say I know the sun will rise tomorrow, because I think of the revolution of the earth as unalterable. I might have said that I know matches are made to strike, and trains go to London, because the working of our civilization seemed unalterable. But, in practice, I cannot be sure of any particular match, or particular train. The match may be badly made; the train may have an 'accident', or I may have been misinformed. Belief, therefore, is a conclusion built on not very positive reasoning. As a reasonable person, the degree of my belief varies with the varying force of my reasons.

Belief is, in substance, an intellectual opinion as to the truth of something. Faith, on the other hand, is a shaping of one's life by trust in someone or something capable of performing what is expected or desired. I might say that I know trains did run through Siberia. I might say I know they do, but perhaps it would be wiser to say I have every belief that they do. But I have faith in those trains, I believe *in* them, only when I mark my letters 'Via Siberia', since otherwise I am not concerned with them.

Faith is not exactly an action. I trust my letters to the post instead of taking them myself. It differs from belief in that it has no degrees at all. I may be very doubtful about the Siberian mail, but I must either write 'Via Siberia' by an act of faith, or let the letter go some other way.

None of these words, however, makes any antithesis to reason. I trust, believe in, have faith in, a doctor, an engineer, or a teacher; in a match, a train, or a watch, because, and so far as, I think it reasonable to trust them. The more I know, the more sure I am about what they can do, the more ready I am to trust them. But I also think it reasonable to trust even when my reason is inadequate to a full comprehension of their methods; very often, just because it is inadequate. If I knew as much as the doctor, I might do my own doctoring. When I no longer trust my watch, I trust it to the watch-maker.

So far I have spoken of faith in its narrowest and simplest forms. If I say that I trust, or have faith in my watch, I mean that I take the time from it without further fussing. But with the cook or my carpenter, it is not quite so simple. I may only mean that I leave the dinner or the axe to them. If, however, I trust the cook or the carpenter personally, as with my friendship, I am trusting them with myself, at least in part. This is a much higher kind of faith, but it is still partial; for even in friendship one does not commit one's whole being. I may, and I do, shrink from committing myself and my life wholly to God, but, just so far as I realize the meaning of God as the Ultimate Purpose, so far I realize that faith in God—if I ever reach it—must come to that.

I have tried to indicate some of the ways in which men's minds reach out in the direction of this faith. I am not sup-posing that anyone begins life with a religion, but we do begin —as I imagine—with a large faith, instinct, assumption, that things are reasonable. Kant would call it a category (or, an 'idea of the reason'). It does not remain, however, a mere assumption. We should not have gone on with it if things had not proved reasonable. As we learnt to find reasons, we learnt to look for them; or, some people did to some degree. It is one of the curiosities of life how little many people care to know reasons. They who seek find, at least in part; for our faith is still a faith. We go on believing that there are reasons even when we cannot find them. That too is good sense. Our knowledge of reasons—which we call understanding—is progressive, and it would not be reasonable, it would be silly, to suppose that the reasonableness of things stopped at the precise point which our knowledge had for the moment reached.

There is no doubt a great deal of silly faith. At times we have all been let down through believing in what was not worth believing. There is also a silly un-belief; for at times we have been left out by not believing in what was worth believing in. Credulous folk, and in-credulous folk, have need of one another; for thus are we all made that it is much easier to see other people's silliness, which we cannot cure, than it is to see our own which, whether we can cure it or not, will have to be paid for.

So far as the mechanism of the world is concerned, our scientific friends gain for us a continually increasing knowledge of processes—of how things go, and can be made to go for our immediate convenience. But that does not tell us anything of the why, of the purpose, of things, and it is with purpose that our own being and life are most concerned. It is in respect of purpose, that this faith of ours, faith in reasonableness, is to us a matter of life and death, intellectually and morally. There is neither sense nor decency to be had without it. We know ourselves as part of a universe. If that universe is a blind mechanism, just so far intelligible that we can make it serve our purposes, yet so utterly unintelligible that there neither are nor can be any purposes except such as we contrive for ourselves, what can this hold out to us but a war of ideals (*Kulturen*)? The same knowledge of mechanism which provides healing provides poison gas? If, however, for 'world-force', we can substitute the name of 'God', as of someone with whom an intelligent soul might reach some measure of understanding, here is a hope for man, and religion is very definitely an expression of that hope.

I have explained already the difficulties which beset our religion. The results are inadequate and unsatisfying, varied, inconsistent, changeable; first, because our experience and our reasoning are incomplete; secondly, and far more seriously, because it is not so much difficult, it is impossible that we should reach God himself; all we can do is to build up a notion or concept of God; or, of what God is 'like'. Further, just because we are so incapable of getting round this impasse, we do not notice it; we assume that the notion of God, since it is all we have, is God himself—all there is of him. And that is the fundamental principle of idolatry.

The confusion here is itself an evasion, but the confusions which come in man's thinking are as nothing to the confusions which follow from his efforts not to think, his efforts to escape the conclusions of his thoughts. Idolatry is one of them. I have alluded to Animism and Pantheism. We will consider now the motive of evasion.

If religion is the deepest expression of all that is in man, there are in us two opposed motives. On the one hand, there is a profound consciousness of our own littleness in face of the world, shown in our dread of what might come upon us from the outside. That fear lies at the root of magic, and the lower forms of religion. On the other hand, there is a not less serious dread of our inner littleness and self-importance. We do want to escape from the pettiness of the self, and the meannesses of its self-ness; yet, at the very same time, mean as we know that self to be, we cling to it passionately, even angrily; for it is all we have. So we cling to our belief in God, to our hope of God, but there are motives in us hardly less strong for wanting to get away from the belief. The anti-idealists—I instanced Voltaire and Hume—admitted the belief was reasonable as to the mere fact of God's existence, but said it could not mean anything, and they said it contemptuously because they were afraid God's existence meant too much. Marcus Aurelius said that you should 'speak respectfully' of Zeus and the universe, although you were only concerned with yourself and your own 'decency'. With heathen religion and 'Zeus'

86

that was possible. Marcus Aurelius just saw the Christian challenge coming, and it frightened him. The English aristocratic, i.e. the public school, attitude is very exactly Stoic. If the Christian challenge gets too insistent, one might be driven to speak of it dis-respectfully, in sheer defence of one's self and its self-right. But it is generally easier to treat religious faith as purely personal, the secret of each man's heart, about which it is good form to say nothing. 'Zeus' meant too little; the Christian creeds mean too much. The 'English' religious reticence is a class habit, which has spread somewhat, though it is not equally felt, outside the circles influenced by the public school spirit.

Those of whom I speak have, as a class, known the Christian faith only from the outside, but the desire to get away from God is universal, common to us religious folk as much as to the non-religious, but our religious evasions are of a much more subtle kind. They are more difficult to meet, and they are more important. Can we really help our friends? Certainly we can hinder them, for the non-religious people are as eager to avail themselves of any excuses we may provide as the mere slackers are to make use of the excuses which quite decent anti-idealists seem to provide.

Let us then face this thought of God, and ask ourselves what we mean by it. There may be evasions, but we will face them also. We shall find them very tempting, and we must see why they tempt us. There may be a good deal of truth in them—otherwise they would hardly be temptations—and whatever truth there is we must recognize and keep. Yet there are hidden dangers which may lead us astray.

There are three main points, or elements, in our thought. We are thinking about an Ultimate of our world; something, that is, beyond the passing and shifting things around us; something eternal on which the changeable rests, from which

87

it comes; something by which—or, I ought to say, here—Someone, to whom, in whose thought and purpose, those things are intelligible. That I called our faith.

By itself it is only a belief that things are that way. It becomes a living faith, the faith of a man's life, by means of hope. The universe is very big, too big for you and me, but if we could reach God, then we also might understand him; at least he would understand us, he would listen to us.

Thirdly, in speaking of God, whatever else we mean, we mean a Reality. (I do not at all like that word. It is too abstract—so is the word Ultimate—but we will let them stand for want of better.) We mean something, or someone, whose purposes and action are as much a matter of fact, as, say, vitamins in animal life, or nitrogen in vegetable life. If you do not know about vitamins and nitrogen, and allow for them, they will not cease to be facts, nor cease to operate. The only difference will be that you will not understand why you are ill, or why your crops are starved.

I made reality my third point, but in fact, it is quite primary. Our faith and hope have no meaning at all apart from it. It is apparently so simple and obvious that we suppose we can take God's existence for granted. Yet to keep it before us is the most difficult thing in life. The thrust and pressure of reality, of things as they are—with that the human soul is ceaselessly struggling, and, in the main, struggling to get away from.

Let us try. 'God is real.' It seems an inspiring thought. What could be plainer?—till one adds—'the Ultimate Will has reality first of all as power', and at that everything in us shrinks. The religious sentiment, or feeling—at least of our modern mind—even revolts. 'God is first of all goodness, love.' The philosophy which is, I believe, most in favour today gives this feeling an intellectual expression, explanation, or justification, in the formula, 'Reality is value', where value plainly means good. We may say that power and goodness are ultimately the same. To be able to say that, really to see them as one, is the very end of religious faith, but at present we are only at the beginning, and in our present state which stands first in our mind?

All of us are, I believe, conscious of these two things in us, which we might call intellect and feeling, or thought and desire. They correspond to faith and hope; they seem, in another way, to correspond to, or to look towards power, about which we think a great deal and might believe in, and goodness, which we desire and hope for. They do not always concur, and it certainly looks as if they might lead us in different directions. In what relation do these stand in our mind? I will discuss the question first quite generally. Later on, we may consider some specific religious teaching which has affected us all a great deal.

Does the reality of God mean to us primarily power, or primarily goodness? I might appeal to Scripture, but I do not think that would be helpful. We shall only start stringing texts against one another, and the people who most need help would not listen at all. They—we—are facing real difficulties. 'Can the Bible, can the Church, can you religious people, meet them?' With a good many—perhaps with most of us, though we do not all recognize it—the question is in fact defiant. So far as it is so, it is no use giving an answer. When people have got into a defiant attitude, they defy the answers. We must meet our difficulties for ourselves; try what answer we can find; think seriously whether what we find is an answer at all. Then, possibly, when we understand our difficulties better, Scripture may help us mightily. That, so far as I can read history, is the road up which God has led mankind; so far as I can read human life, that seems to be the road by which God leads you and me.

To our immediate question, our philosophic friends gave us a suggestion—'Reality is value.' It is not for us to argue with philosophers. We must try to understand them—if we can—and what we learn we must use. But I think this maxim, in the form we get it, is going to be very difficult. When I was in Japan, I heard there was a war on. A bit ago there was a total eclipse at 6 a.m. In my room someone left a bucket, where in the dark, I might run against it. I have always supposed these things 'really' were, or happened, though I do not think most people had any value for them. The young lady (in *Punch*) said, 'Wasn't the darling Corona just too sweet', but I do not imagine that her, or even the astronomers', fervent appreciation affected the eclipse notably. In England, I believe, it did not even make the eclipse visible. Values do not make things. It is true that, so far as we can, we do make things to have value. Some people made a war, and some of us have made other things. Very often we wish we hadn't, but that, alas, will not un-make them.

Certainly in our ordinary and common way of talking, reality belongs to what is capable of doing something, of producing real results. When Dr Johnson kicked the leg of the table (or, was it a stone?), he seems to have been saying that it was real enough to stop his foot moving. Someone dislikes our using the word reality, because so many of us mean only the material. I am afraid some of us do talk that way when we are puzzled, rather cross, and argumentative, but I never met any common folk who seriously thought that only the material was real. It is equally true that a number—a larger number—of people habitually talk of values as cash values. I do not think they mean it either. I was told that some officers in the war argued that victory was all a material matter of shells, but they knew quite well that the provision of shells required forethought, and that the use of shells involved skill, discipline, courage, in the gunners. All these qualities are very real and they are not material. Napoleon said that the moral forces in war were to the material as three to one.

I think the fact is that in the experience of our life, we find the two sides so associated that we get a bit restless and puzzled when people seem to oppose them. We have no difficulty over material things, because they always do something, if only adding weight or mass. We are not so sure about mental things, notably about theories. Suppose there were idealists who thought that 'justice' would by itself prevent war or win it. That would be a real theory in that it might produce real consequences—viz., unpreparedness. The officers who were practical people, and who knew what being shelled feels like, might call it a mere theory, or even an un-real theory, because it was out of relation to facts, and would not produce the intended consequences.

I have discussed this question of reality at some length for various reasons: first, because, even if we are not good thinkers, we must keep somewhere in touch with solid think-ing, and have some notion of how we use the word reality; secondly, because, when we do, we can get a little light on the perplexing difference between idealists and practical people, and it is a very disastrous thing indeed if our Christian faith turns out to be a Gospel only to the rich—in ideals. I have always understood that it was a Gospel especially to the poor. Above all, however, I want to make clear how this question of reality applies to our religion. I said above that we religious folk had no doubt at all that our faith and hope were addressed to Someone real, and yet that the reality of God was in-conceivably difficult to keep to; it is so difficult to face.

From all we have ever said or felt or meant, looking to

the reality of God and for the sake of our faith, we must ask, we cannot help asking—What does God do? What is he doing? We may ask, but the question is very big. Perhaps we cannot answer; indeed, I do not see how we can expect to answer. There is, however, another question much simpler about which we must make up our minds one way or another: Does God do anything? or, is God only a name for ideals, an assumed source of ideals? Is God's purpose something which he is himself carrying out—that is what I meant by power— or only something which he would very much like to have, but is powerless to effect, and wishes we should carry through for him.

I am not asking a merely theoretical, but a very urgent, question. Certain people in the eighteenth century admitted that God—'the Supreme Being'—was the only possible cause for a universe, but that only concerned 'a theory of origins'. In practice God had nothing further to do with the universe. However the universe got here, we have to live in it as we best can. We call that Deism. But a great many highly ortho- dox people have spoken of the moral law in just the same way. God is its only possible source. Being religious people, they believed he would reappear on pay-day, but in the mean- time he has gone away, 'left us', to carry out the moral law. I should call this moral Deism. It is a quite common religious position. (A) 'Left us', is an actual quotation. A distinguished preacher—a bishop, several years before the war—said (B) 'God must be nearly heart-broken at the way things are going on.' In a church paper from the other side of the world I saw it quoted, as a remarkable suggestion, without any demur. Another speaker put it to a large, and, one would have ex- pected, a critical audience, (C) 'We must not take evil as an argument against the being of God. God is doing his best.' It was admitted by implication that he was not making much of it. The audience was not critical; audiences seldom are. So far as I can gather on such occasions, pious folk only put their heads a little on one side, and said, 'Ah, how true!' (I have lettered these quotations because we shall want them again.)

Here I venture to issue a word of warning. We religious people, in spite of our idealism, are in our own fashion intensely practical folk. We do not like philosophy because it sounds, perhaps is, a bit too abstract and theoretical for us. Our danger is that so long as statements, platitudes such as I have quoted, sound nice, so long as they stir our aforesaid feelings, we do not stop to think what they mean or involve; it does not occur to us that we may be glossing over our difficulties and our needs, and that under pious phraseology, we are substituting un-belief for belief. If you do not see what that means, or how it could be possible, let me remind you of a well-known story. Once upon a time, there was a religious institution which called itself 'the Catholic Church'. It had developed a very complete system of religious practices. There arose a man, called Luther, who said, 'Without knowing it, you have substituted un-belief for belief; belief in the works of men for faith in God.' The Catholics were naturally indignant, and presently retorted the charge: 'You Protestants are substituting un-belief for belief—belief in your own judgment and in your own feelings for belief in the teaching and gift of God.' I offer no decision on either accusation. I only point out that both parties believed that such substitutions were possible and very disastrous, though neither would believe that he might himself be making a substitution. If I may repeat a favourite saying: 'With all thy learning learn scepticism, but especially scepticism of yourself and of what appeals to you.' Scepticism of other folk's notions comes by nature, and does not need learning. You are not responsible for other folk, and it is doubtful if you can mend them, though you may try. Self-criticism, on the other hand, is an effective sign of humility, which is reckoned to be a Christian virtue.

We are at this point plainly involved in the old difficulty of omnipotence. We old-fashioned orthodox (I am only a middle Victorian myself) considered ourselves bound by the doctrine of omnipotence. I suppose the bishop (cf. *B*) would have admitted as much, yet he plainly evades it. It is possible to say, some do say, God is omnipotent but self-limited, in particular by the gift of free will. One way or another, so far as our life is concerned and for all its practical purposes, God is not omnipotent. The modern mind does not like evasions, and rejects the doctrine of omnipotence positively. 'If God is omnipotent, why does he not stop the war?' said the bored soldier, and being bored is worse than being frightened; it goes on so much longer. Being frightened might lead to prayer; being bored leads to nothing. I am afraid we middle Victorians were very self-satisfied in our time, yet there was a great deal we never saw. However, I am not going to reject omnipotence in a hurry lest I lose something, but then neither will I be in a hurry to reject the rejections, lest I miss learning something. Are we not all a little too much in a hurry, and, therefore, too sure?

'I hope I am not keeping you too long,' said the preacher, whereupon the congregation, which had been really interested, began to yawn and look at its watches. I am going to follow my own line. We are up against a very big question, which covers all the meaning, all the contradictions—and I would say the absurdities—of our life. I said there was an answer; but I will not give it, and it would be no use giving it, till we have worked our way through the questions. Here also we must not be in a hurry. No book can give you an answer. You, and your soul, and God Almighty, will have to fight it out, will go on fighting it out, pretty well as long as your life lasts. I am more or less trying to tell you how or why it is such a tangled business. If I show you the tangles, I am not making it tangled, but the knots come pretty much in this order: we felt the world, and we felt after God, as something better than, and above the world. And we thought we were sure that God was real, but reality means power, effectiveness. Then we were rather doubtful, and wanted to get out of it, partly because we were involved in another knot—the age-long problem of evil.

What is evil? St Augustine said it had no reality at all. All being was good, and evil was a defect, like a man having lost an arm. St Augustine was a very great man, but I feel about this as I feel about values. It is rather difficult to follow. No doubt evil is essentially destructive, and so negative, but then destructiveness is as much a positive or real activity as construction. The war was horribly destructive, it was also horribly real. And there are a good many destructive things like the ichneumon fly—which lays its eggs in the living caterpillar, and which puzzled Darwin so much. There are the malarial germs, and many more such. Is death not a reality? The struggle with evil is a very real factor in our life. We all take it so, and we do not struggle against unreal things. In the old days, religion as the expression of what men could find in the world, had to express and allow for evil as well as good. The magic-worship addressed to spirits, the confusions of polytheism, the philosophic dualism of Zoroaster (Persia), with its theory of two Creators, good and evil, struggling against one another, are partly efforts to explain; in result, they only confess and re-state, the facts seen.

To our modern mind, this heathen attitude is intolerable. Evil cannot be an eternal principle, therefore it cannot have

95

place in God. But what is our alternative? I gave three quotations. Two of them (*A* and *B*) seem to involve what I called moral Deism. God has ideals and is presumably keen about them, but he has nothing to do with the actual state of affairs which we manage well or ill as we can or choose. The third quotation (*C*) allows that God does something—'his best'—it is not clear how, nor what it amounts to.

These quotations are from orthodox speakers, who did not, as I imagine, quite realize what they were saying. Possibly they did, possibly they even explained, but the words, as quoted, express a somewhat vague craving in our minds. There is, however, a quite definite theory, which has taken immense hold on the modern mind. Kant maintained that we know 'things-in-themselves' only according to the fashion of our own ideas or 'experience', but then we are not concerned with things in themselves, but only with things as they affect us. By 'practical reason', by taking them according to our ideas, we get the results we want well enough, whether in religion, morality, or science.

About 1860, Ritschl reverted to Kant. Pure truth was of merely intellectual interest, and belonged to 'metaphysics' in which he included 'cosmology', theories, that is, of the universe, of whether it existed of itself or was created by intelligence. We were not concerned with the universe; we were concerned with ourselves, with our own personal life or 'experience', determined not by abstract judgments of truth, but by judgments as to value. Some of his followers (Hermann) maintained that judgments as to value were as much a matter of the intellect or reason as any other judgments, but the general tendency in religious circles is to insist that feeling is more primary and more fundamental than reason (so Otto), and that judgments of value primarily belong to feeling, some would say to the will also, though perhaps reason may come in as a secondary matter. Here the two spheres of theology and religion mark themselves off.

This language—about the contrast of theology and religion, about value-judgments and religious experience—has become enormously popular. It is the more curious that so few people, other than professed students, have heard of Ritschl, but the system was welcomed because it seemed to offer, as it was intended to offer, an easy escape from the troublesome questions of philosophy and science, of historical and other criticism, all which we may safely leave to anyone interested in such abstruse subjects. They do not affect the value of our religious feeling and experience. In result, modern religion has tended to take its place as a branch of psychology. It can hardly be said, I think, that this system does anything to meet the practical problem of evil, but at least it has put the difficulty of evil outside religion.

I do not want to be unsympathetic towards any honest attempt to meet difficulties, especially one which appeals to so many earnest people. I do not think a good many of us realize how much it appeals, not merely to professed 'modernists' whom we might suspect of hunting for a novel theory, but to all. Newman's attitude to reason is not unlike Kant's, though I believe he knew nothing of Kant. Many trenchantly orthodox priests, and an uncounted multitude also of laity, maintain the same sharp contrast between intellectualism and devotional values, between theology and religion, without having been influenced by Ritschl even indirectly. His views may be to us of no importance at all, but he has formulated rather carefully what we shrink from formulating, and it is worth our while to see whether our difficulties can be met in this way, or are only being evaded.

In this system two very main questions—(i) the question of truth, and (ii) the question of the world—are avowedly set on one side. Its attitude to (iii) the reality of God is not quite so clear. But, if we take these two troublesome questions about truth and the world out of our religion, have we thereby got rid of them from our lives? Have we done more than confess that religion cannot help us to deal with them? Let us see what is involved in each.

(1) *Truth.* We religionists are for the most part very simple folk. We do know that our religion is to us a thing of great value. We are a little afraid of reason, intellectualism, and metaphysics, and of where they may lead us. Nevertheless, if Ritschl says—what critics of all kinds had said before—'By all means stick to your religious feelings, and the critics will not trouble you if you will admit that your religion has nothing to do with truth'—then our conscience revolts. The price for such easy evasions is much too high.

(*a*) Long before Kant and Ritschl, politicians, religionists, and everybody realized that the truth of things is too big and complex for our limited reason and imagination, but we have no doubt it exists. If we cannot reach the truth—save in bits, with great difficulty, and some uncertainty—it is constantly reaching us at the most unexpected and inconvenient moments. 'Watch! For it is in such an hour as you are not thinking of it that the most tremendous of all reality comes on you.'

(*b*) There is the same distinction between ultimate values and values as we estimate them, that there is between the real truth and what we believe to be true, but there is a very serious difference in our handling of the two conceptions. In all ordinary affairs, when a man talks of truth, he is always supposed to be talking of something positive and unalterable. Neither he nor anyone imagines that what he thinks or says makes the thing so or not so, happen or not happen. It is only perhaps in religious matters that we confuse the two, and talk of a belief being 'true for him', because he thinks it true. When a man talks of value, he is quite commonly supposed to be talking relatively to himself. My fountain-pen is what it is for anybody; its value to me, and its value to anyone else are quite different.

I take it as a condition of all sanity that our estimates of good shall be held secondary to the question of fact and truth. I mean secondary in the proper sense; I do not mean less important. Natural science seems to me the sanest thing we have, because in its practice, not always in its philosophy, it sticks solidly to this faith in a reality which we learn as we can, though its truth always reaches out beyond our knowledge, which afterwards we use as we may according to its value for our purposes. I take it as no less a condition of moral honesty. Bossuet calls it 'the worst aberration of the human intellect to believe that things are so, because we should like them to be so'; that is, because we put that value on them.

(2) *The World-problem.* Is it possible for us to treat the world-problem as outside our religion? Ritschl, regarding Christianity as 'the most highly developed religion', did not think heathen religions worth considering at all. Thereby he failed to observe, what seems to me the plain fact, that men always have been wrestling with a world-problem, though their notions of a world were more often practical than philosophic. It is not as a metaphysician, nor as a cosmologist, but as a very average person that I believe I can answer for others. Probably most people find the world much more interesting than their own personalities; their duties in the world appeal to them much more than the contemplation of their own inner states. They may be wrong, but in the face of a certain text about those who 'love their own soul' or psyche, who

99

think too much of their own psychology, I should hesitate to say they were wholly wrong.

Some devout religionists in every age have tried to set aside the world for religious self-concentration. The Puritans, the Moravians, the Lutheran pietists, the early Evangelicals separated sharply between the inner life and worldliness. Long before any of them, to escape the world-problem, men fled to monasticism, and called it 'religion', exactly as Ritschl does. I believe all these people were so far bearing a true witness that an answer to the world-problem cannot be found in the world. Yet the results proved that it is not possible to escape the world. A good many—perhaps I—would right gladly let the world alone if it would let me alone, and it never will. The early monks were hermits, but the Church, for good reasons, discouraged that form of life. The community constituted a world in which a man had to learn to live with others, and the community had property. I will not discuss the theory of religious individualism at this point, but it remains as of Christian faith, that God who *made* the world, so *loved* the world.

(3) *Concerning God.* I do not think we need trouble further with Ritschl's views. After that verse we have reached something of our own. God, truth, the world—these three things stand together in our mind indisseverably, but they come to us in the opposite order. The world and the things of the world are continually thrusting themselves, unbidden, upon our experience. We have our own notions of the world; very absurd some of them may be. Is it possible for us to know the truth of the world? Scientists have found out many bits of truth, some mighty useful for our bits of purposes, but the real whole truth, on which a real whole life should be built, we cannot know, though it is that real whole truth which most matters, and which we long to know.

Here I think we may get a glimpse of our end. The difficulty has been this; the truth of fact is an assumption of something beyond us—a faith, a hope, a dream, a guess; what we have, what constitutes our actual world, is in itself a chaos of discordant experiences within us. The reality of truth and the reality of experience, therefore, stand apart, and the unreconciled contradiction jeers at all our attempts to bring them together. We try to find an *interpretation* of experience within the compass of such ideals and theories as are possible to us, but it is presently plain that the interpretative ideals and theories are as discordant as the experiences. That is our dualism; I now add—'but all reality is a Trinity.' If there is a truth of things whole, if it is more than a dream and a way of talking, that truth is in God, who also made us and the world. If we can bring together, not the two factors, but these three, they make sense. Nothing else does.

God, truth, the world—I am not speaking of the divine Trinity, though I have come very near it, but of a trinity of human experience, which makes a unity of life, as dualism makes its dis-unity. I take experience as the substance of human life, but there is an ambiguity about the word so puzzling that most of us never notice it at all. Ordinarily, by an experience, one means an experience of things, as of objects outside oneself. A man of considerable experience means a man who has seen, come across, a great many things. I came across a bucket in the dark. I suppose, I daresay, the experience actually consisted in certain feelings in me—pain, annoyance, and so on—but I ordinarily think of these feelings as arising from an object which I failed to notice. In our modern psychological religion, experience seems to be not infrequently spoken of, and treated, as if the feelings existed of themselves, and had value in themselves, without regard to any object— as experiences of an experience, or, if you prefer, as an experience of certain feelings. No doubt feelings can and do exist in that fashion. A good many of us know the experience of feeling cross, or feeling a grievance—when there is no available object to justify the feeling. I believe we are all agreed that such feelings are morbid, and rather absurd. Out of sheer self-respect we look round carefully to find someone to be cross with, or something to grouse over. Another way, of course, is to bid your feelings do what they are told, and clear out when they are not wanted. If they won't—as often they won't—you can let them alone till they wither on their neglected stalks. There are advantages in this method. They will learn better next time.

Sometimes, no doubt, feelings are apparently the most important part of an experience. I have always understood, first, that the attraction of sports lay in the feeling of mastery over the situation presented, but especially over yourself, that is over your other feelings; and, secondly, that the true value of sports lay in the effect of this self-mastery upon character. Moralists often talk as if that meant control of your temper, which young boys and some others learn with difficulty. But that is a very elementary matter. To the normal sportsman the effort required is much more complex. On the one hand, if, or when, a real batsman lets the joy of hitting gain the mastery over him, he will get out. On the other hand—I speak more confidently for the rabbit—if he cannot control his fear of getting out, he will never do anything at all. For here is the paradox—the ostensible objects of the player—runs, goals, or what not—are quite secondary both to the joy and to the value of the game; nevertheless, if the player does not keep his attention fixed on the lesser matter of making runs and so forth, the resultant experience is not likely to be soothing to his feelings, nor will it give uplift to his character.

What happens in sport happens more or less everywhere. If you will take your business seriously, with an honest reverence for its purpose and the proper ways thereto, you will get all the feelings which are good either for you or your character ('fun in bucketsful'). If you go after feelings and character, you will probably be first bored, and in the latter end thereof a prig. I said that at the start, and imagined that as a platitude it was acceptable. We took the rotter to be a man who saw no purpose, who contemplated life as a joy-ride, where you get sensations simply by buzzing along, although there is no idea of going anywhere, indeed, nowhere to go to. It is on just this ground that we distinguish sport from serious business. In sport, the professed object is not its real value, though even here the sportsman must treat it as if it were. In serious business there is no question that the true value belongs to the object or purpose.

And now—what is religion? A worship of God? But what is God, and why should we worship? Is religion of the nature of a sport, and are we to worship God, not because God can do anything, but because it gives us such beautiful feelings, and so much uplift, to talk as if he could. Is this a sarcasm? I mean it as a warning. We have every need to test what we are saying and what appeals to us, by trying what it can look like in blunt and vulgar language. I have known quite a number of religious people argue openly that the value of prayer was subjective. Plainly, they did not think God did anything, anyhow it made no difference asking him, except that it was very good for them to talk as if it did make this difference. The mere suggestion of such subjectivism horrifies us, makes us indignant. By all means let us go on being horrified, but I do not think it is wise to be indignant. There is a great deal more in all of us than we care to recognize, and the real horror of this subjectivism, of this horizon-notion that we all are the real or the effective centre of things—is that it is so near to us, and so difficult to escape.

On the other hand, I do not say that religion is the business of life, I urge that it is concerned with the business of life. We worship God, seek after God, because we recognize that he is, that what he does is, much the biggest and most real factor in life. We can make no sense of our own life, nor of the world we have to deal with, unless we recognize that their meaning and purpose lie with him. We can take prayer as the most typical act of religion. I am very conscious of the difficulty of explaining prayer. I do not think we are quite ready for an explanation yet, but at least men always have prayed, and certainly they did so in all simplicity because they felt, believed, or assumed, that God could do something. I repeat now a point I put forward in Chapter I. Religion is the most central of all human activities, but since it is an activity of ours, the worship of religion is a worship of the self, no doubt of the higher self. This worship of religion is constantly, most easily, very disastrously, confused with, yet it obscures and displaces, the worship of God, which is plainly a very different thing.

V

EVIL, SIN, AND THE SELF

W E have in our minds, then, two thoughts of God, not at first very different, but they tend to draw apart, as we struggle to bring them together. In the first place, God is to us the Ultimate Cause or Creator not of things only, but of ideals also; not merely a dead cause in the past, nor merely the originator of a moral code. He is an efficient present cause. That I called the substance of our faith, which is a looking *to* Someone beyond all the insufficiency of our measure. In the second we look to him also as the Ultimate, where all good and all values rest. That is the basis of our hope; since hope is a looking *for* a good which may come to us. Faith and hope are also not quite identical, yet cannot be separated.

And now what is good? In what relation does this Ultimate Good stand towards good as we think of it, judge or measure it? All reasonable people recognize that our judgments of value are often wrong, and at best tentative. On the other hand, good must mean something to us; it must be possible somehow to recognize good as good. If we are to use the word at all, we cannot treat it as a mere label. This ambiguity (1) it will take all the rest of this chapter to start unravelling; (2) we shall be occupied all the rest of our lives struggling with it; and (3) it is the peace of the world to come that we shall be at home in; for then we shall see face to face, what now we see in a glass darkly—how to understand what God does and to bring our judgment into accord with his.

But, if we know where to look, I think we may learn something even now.

Early in the last chapter we found ourselves, not for the first time, confronted by the problem of evil. I did not mean to evade it, but it got shoved on one side by the problem of reality and the world. Now, however, we will take it up properly. If from God all good comes, does not evil also come from God? Here also we will have sections.

I *Evil in Nature*

We will deal first with evil in nature, which I do not think there is any possibility of denying. An early Victorian orthodoxy sheltered itself by arguing that perhaps good did not mean the same in God that it does with us. I do not know very well what was meant by this; it looks rather like using a label. Anyhow John Stuart Mill answered; 'There is nothing men count evil and abominable—cruelty, moral indifference, the infliction of pain and death—which Nature does not habitually practise. If I am to go to hell unless I call evil good, to hell I will go.' The passage has been often quoted and much admired. To me the second sentence seems a little too self-conscious, too flamboyant, to be convincing. However, it has an honesty we should imitate.

Pain. The facts we have to face are, in the first place, physical pain and physical death. We cannot help recognizing, but we must not exaggerate, the evil. Pain, in particular, is to an enormous extent a matter of imagination, of anticipation and reflection, which constitute sensitiveness. And we know, even amongst men, how variable that is. In the lower animals —such as the caterpillar devoured by the ichneumon grub— there is certainly the appearance of pain, but with such a very simple nerve system, what does it amount to? Even the higher animals do not feel pain as we do, because they do not brood over it. People who are habituated, say, to mosquitoes, hardly notice them.

Let us for the moment go on to the more direct question of physical death. Is death an evil? For the individual—certainly it is; final evil. I suppose I must say so, though I do not feel entirely convinced. It rather sets me wondering whether there is any very solid meaning for an individual good. This is a 'good' tree and growing well, but is it evil that so few acorns ever get a chance? The pigs eat a good many. The swallow is a thing of beauty, and it eats a lot of flies. We have plenty to spare in summer in this place. If you do not drown your kittens, they will starve, and an over-stocked rabbit-warren is not a cheery sight. Nature works out a great whole order, by a method we call natural selection. Number and multiplication involve strife, and birth involves death.

II *Moral Evil*

I do not profess to have disposed of the problem of pain, but however perplexing, it is yet secondary. At most it proves —perhaps it does prove—that there is evil *in* nature. But what are we to say where we find the whole order of things based on, made out of, these three factors—birth, death, and a struggle which can have but the one ending. It is this great law of strife which seems to us so terrible—in the strict sense of the word, it frightens us by suggesting that the order of nature is itself evil. It seems contrary to all our moral conceptions. My quotation from Mill makes that plain. He calls certain things evil, which perhaps they are. He also calls them abominable—which is a moral judgment. And the 'moral indifference' of nature is made a grave count. It was so with the soldiers in the war. Something might be said for a moral government if 'luck' were served out according to moral desert. It weighs with us all. The hawk seeks his dinner, and he strikes most commonly at the bird which is slowest, least alert, perhaps oldest. Possibly, if he would do the policeman and confine himself to birds of criminal habits—cuckoos for instance—our magistrate-conscience might grant the dinner as earned.

It still remains that we must not confuse our factual judgments as to how things are and what comes of them, with our moral judgments as to how things ought to be. Only when we have faced facts honestly, we can also claim that moral values, the facts of value, are not less real than material facts. But, for reasons I gave in the last chapter, that contention involves us in its own difficulties. Certainly the moral ideal is appealing to what is best in us. We must learn to see things as they are, but the worship of things as they are is degrading. When I say—there are two sides, and this is a very important side; I mean just that, and I am not going back from it, because I also press the other, perhaps less welcome side.

And the less welcome side is this—that it is just in regard to values that our self-assertion is most in evidence. We often find it difficult to face facts quite squarely, but we resent any notion of a difference in moral judgments though we know people do differ about them. I am allowed to say that our estimates of good are not the same as Ultimate Good so long as I leave the platitude in the 'Ah! how true' stage. If I press it in any practical form, I shall not be popular. But have we altogether lost desire for an understanding between our idealist selves and 'practical' folk? For the sake of that understanding I am willing to risk my popularity.

There is an important distinction between the ideas of good or evil and of right or wrong. Good and evil are not necessarily moral words at all. This is a good horse, and the batsman makes a good score, which is bad for the bowler's average. In the moral sense, the words are relative, applicable to a man's character, motives, essentially to ideals, as more or less worthy —worth more. Right and wrong are positives, applicable legally to a man's actions, as they do or do not accord with a code, standard, or law.

These codes vary enormously according to the different forms of society in which people live. The *Jungle Book* gives us the code of the wolf-pack. There is a very strict code of the blood-feud, as there was of the duel. There is a code among schoolboys. Most of these codes—like the code of business—accept the struggle for existence as a normal condition of living—sometimes with a crude delight. The old saga heroes killed one another joyously, but they only did to their neighbours what they would their neighbour should do to them. They expected to get killed, wanted to be killed; for to die in your bed was 'a cow's death', and the fighting man out-West wished to 'die in his boots'. Whatever the fashion of life might be, the code made association in a common life possible by maintaining certain qualifications as to how far you might go, rules as to what is or is not 'sporting'.

Ideals, however, underlie all codes, shaping the life for which the codes provide rules, just as our ideas of God shape our religious practices. What I called 'purposes' are the active side of ideals. In my middle Victorian days morals were assumed to be quite plain, in contrast with Religion, about which people never would agree. Fifty years has made a great difference. Just as the new generation awakes to the difficulty of finding any ideal for life, so it becomes contemptuous of the moral 'conventions' which no longer seem to have a meaning. I hope I need not, frankly I dare not, attempt to describe what this moral revolt leads to, both in this country and in America, where I am told it is even more marked. I have just had an advertisement of a new novel. 'The book is frankly unconventional.' I forget how many thousands it has sold.

I stand to all I have said throughout. We idealists must bear our witness before the world to the truth and reality of purpose and religion, of the ideals and values of life. I am not going back on that because I am also contending that the truth and reality of these values is something far greater than can be comprehended in our life, or in our measure. If we do not recognize the difficulties and contradictions of our own littleness, we destroy all the effectiveness of our witness; for we are pointing people in directions where they very well know that these things will not be found. And it is to me rather appalling how astonishingly certain many of us are, not merely that truth and value exist for life, but that we know exactly what they are, and how they should be estimated.

The world holds such a lot of people. Some, soft-handed, timid, and a bit comfortable—I am one; some rough-handed, venturesome—soldiers, police, navvies, pioneers. Some of us think, dream dreams, and do psycho-analysis; some—business men, politicians, and so forth—bustle things along, struggling with practical difficulties, of which I know little, except that I am sure I could not meet them. I want, we all want, to help these people to see more of the glory that is about them, the glory of the work God has given them to do. I know a great many of us are helping far more effectively than I can. At the same time, in a multitude of books I seem to find a really astonishing confidence in judging other people's ideals, or lack of ideals; for in our ethical, in our religious, as in our political, controversies the difficulty is to realize that the other man has an ideal at all.

It is so with the people round us, and it is the same with

the past. We estimate and judge with entire serenity concerning the ethical outlook and teaching of patriarchs and kings, prophets and psalmists, even apostles and evangelists; for only their ethical outlook and teaching have value for us, though, for my part, I find it hard to realize what value they can have when we are already ethically competent to dictate these discriminating estimates. As to later times—popes and bishops, saints and martyrs, doctors and monks—it is not easy to understand what they were trying to do, but there is no doubt that it is not only within our competence, it is our duty, to pronounce the judgment of 'modern ethical standards' on them and all they did do. We have no need to wait for the Parousia. The Day of Judgment has already come. Is it the Last Judgment? I think it must be; for we not only demand an 'ethical concept of God', we can determine exactly what it should contain, that is, what God can or can not be allowed to do. And, if that is not the last, I do not know what judgment we can go on to.

Brothers dear, where have we got to? What does it all mean? Are we so entirely lords of all things that it is up to us to grant God a place in his own universe if he can bring a good character? Is the Gospel message nothing more than this: that 'God is niceness, and in him is nothing nasty at all'? If so, are we not making God in our own image? And this God, whom we have constructed, measured, remodelled, according to our estimates, in what possible sense can we say that we believe in him? Surely it is for him to believe in us.

Some may think that my account of our self-confident judgments is exaggerated, although every phrase in it is a reminiscence, a quotation, a summary, of things I have met over and over again. For my part I am more struck with its inevitableness, and the difficulty of avoiding it. It is claimed and I claim that we are meant and ought to judge; certainly we do judge and we believe, and must believe, that our judgments have a real validity. If we believe that God is good, that constitutes a judgment. Is good the same as niceness? In using our judgment, it seems as if we only could come out more or less at this point, which certainly looks startling, not to say preposterous. But is our judgment final? May not our judgment constitute a judgment on ourselves? In the end do we judge God, or does God judge us?

III *Sin*

We have struggled with the problem of evil, first, of physical evil in nature, virtually in the form of pain. But I pointed out, secondly, that real trouble was not with physical evil, but with the apparent immoralism, of nature. And we resent it for the reason I gave that, in spite of Ritschl, the world-order, which we call nature, will not let us alone. It thrusts itself into our life in the teeth of our ideals, and we resent it the more because so many people seem satisfied with it.

I do not want to be unsympathetic, but I do ask for a little quiet self-criticism. When one looks at those all too confident judgments, is it not plain that our self-assertion is confusing people rather than helping? We tug at our knots rather fiercely because we have missed something, and, therefore, do not understand.

The first point is very simple. Monks, Puritans, and pietists are bearing a true witness that this evil of nature shall not 'have dominion over us.' That is a very serviceable text, but plainly we must not argue that the only way to escape 'dominion' is to reject use. I do not mean to judge the splendid devotion of these people, but are we meant to imitate them? They did what they could. The alabaster vase was well worth breaking, but it is not given as the only way of service.

The second point goes much deeper. Physical evil and moral evil, evil in nature and evil in men—where does this moral evil come from? Why do men do such things? And we ask with a certain indignation; for we think of moral evil, not solely, but primarily, mainly, fundamentally, as something which other people do. (I know that will be resented, but I will come back to it.) No wonder we are perplexed. We shall not understand that evil till we recognize and try to understand it in ourselves. Evil in men must be a personal evil, evil somehow in a will, in a *me*. This personal evil is what some call sin.

Now sin is a very ugly name for a very ugly thing, and we do not like ugliness, especially when we do not know what to do about it. The whole idea and doctrine of sin is intensely unpopular; we all feel we are being hit or going to be hit. We try to evade it in every way. There is nowhere that we need so much, or that I plead so hard for, patience and self-criticism; there is nowhere that we so much need, and that I so plead for, the facing of facts, even if they are ugly and perplexing facts.

(1) Some modern writers minimize the importance of sin altogether. Maybe twenty years ago a distinguished professor wrote a very remarkable saying: 'The modern man is not worrying over his sins. His business is to be up and doing.' These remarkable sayings puzzle me. They are often, as here, so true and so revealing, yet their authors do not always seem to recognize, nor do readers ask, what they reveal. There have always been quite a large number of people, as far back as Old Testament times, who did not worry over their sins—another recent theologian called them 'healthy-minded'—but

I never felt special admiration for them. Generally speaking, it is easy enough to forget one's own sins; it is other people's sins which worry us. Yet not even that is intellectually satisfying. 'The other man' must be a *me* somewhere.

(2) A very distinguished writer—Mr Tennant of Cambridge, explains sin as an 'anachronism'—the welling up of primitive instincts, which are now out of place, and should have been outgrown. The explanation seems a little thin. It applies to certain obvious sins, such as losing one's temper, the sins, in general, of disreputable people. But when one rises into a controlled, un-primitive, more artificial, state, is one really a better man? Children are deplorably anachronous; adults are much further from the primitive, yet a well-known saying begins: 'Except ye become as little children'—I might paraphrase it 'the kingdom of heaven is open both to adults and children but only on exactly the same terms.'

(3) It seems fixed in all our minds that sin is essentially an act—of the will. We think of it legally as an indictable, or statable offence, as though we were in a law court. Mr Tennant says emphatically that 'Sin is only a rhetorical phrase for sins.' And to a good many religious people 'an act done against the commandments of God', is the accepted or stock definition. It has seemed to me curious; for, when I replied: 'Sin is first selfishness; then, separation from God', they always assent. But selfishness and separation describe certain tendencies, motives, attitudes of the soul. Selfishness is a cause of certain acts; separation may be a result of acts. Neither is 'an act'. As to Mr Tennant, I would no more confuse sin, as a state of the soul, with the sins one commits, than I would confuse thought, which is a certain activity of the mind, with the thoughts which the mind produces.

(4) When I said that to us moral evil means primarily what somebody else does, I know it sounds nasty and sarcastic.

In fact it is inevitable. A man has certain moral ideals. To have ideals and to think them right ideals is the same thing. The ideals a man condemns as positive evil only can be somebody else's. He can only condemn himself for not acting up to his ideals. In quite common language, 'We are well aware of our many failings and imperfections, which we greatly regret,' though I doubt if we care to know too much about them, and we are quite sure other people are wrong when they think they know.

I need not go on with these theories. Certain things are evident. Evil or sin in us cannot be primarily acts, since acts are not primary. They are my acts. If they are wrong, it is I who am wrong; and the wrongness, or sin, in me perverts what I do; it may pervert even my good acts. No one would say that prayer and almsgiving could be wrong in themselves, but they may be, as our Lord showed, very wrong indeed as we do them.

I should have said, everybody is conscious of this wrong in himself. If I may quote the Prayer Book, it seems to feel that to come to prayer at all—daily, morning and evening, most of all when you come to the presence of God Given— you should first confess that 'there is no health (wholeness or salvation) in us,' and 'the burden is intolerable.' I know that many people regard that language as exaggerated. My 'theologian' above is quoting Professor James' idea that the strong sense of sin seen in St Paul, St Augustine, and Luther, belongs to 'twice-born souls'. It is a sheer fact to be faced that people differ immensely in sensibility, as in capacity, for ideals, for thought, and many other things, but the notion of any *radical* difference between rich and poor, upper and lower classes, in any respect whatever, fills me with horror. The distinction I do see is between men, who have faced the sense of sin—not always primarily, but always ultimately—because they have found the answer to it; and those who, because they did not know how to face it, have fallen back on the sufficiency of being comfortable and respectable. Some may be comfortably satisfied, a good many assert they are; but they leave me unconvinced. I know many others, apparently 'healthy-minded', who know quite well that they are wrong. I do not know if any of them will read this book or think anything of it, but I am thinking of them.

What then is this evil in us, persisting as a universal element, in spite of all our desire for goodness? Why cannot we, why cannot even the best of us, get rid of it; for strangely enough the best are most conscious of it, and our conscience tells us that they are right, and that self-satisfaction is not only a sin, but a folly, a falsity?

Of course, human nature has its own specific limitations or imperfections, but it would be absurd to speak of it as evil. I am not evil because I am a man, but because I am a poor sort of man. Evil is in men, in us, in me. Now I will state the consequence quite definitely and we will see what we can make of it.

The actual principle of evil which we call sin, not only is in me; it is the *me*, the self. That is what theologians call original sin, something born in us and unescapable, as the very condition of our life.

The doctrine of original sin is none the more popular for being 'orthodox', but I need not argue about that.

'If the sin is unescapable, why should we be blamed?' Why, indeed? I am not talking about blame; I am talking about the facts of our life, though I think we might be blamed for refusing to face them.

'But is it a fact? How can the self be sin?' In reply, I think I can borrow a fairly simple explanation, which may help. Then I will just point out shortly—if it is not already plain—

how the contradictions and perplexities of life, which I have only been setting out on paper, all obviously arise from this contradiction of the self. With that the purely human part is finished, and we can set our mind towards God and to the Gospel, where the escape lies from all these negations.

Professor W. James, writing as a psychologist, not as a religionist, points out a certain law: 'Everything comes before us as a fragment torn out of a whole.' Your attention picks out, say, a flower from its background; colours are known by contrast; sciences abstract particular aspects—the mechanical, chemical, and so on—out of a complex thing, event, phenomenon. I might go on to apply his law to logic, philosophy, politics, history; it applies, as he says, to 'everything'. We do not always realize it, because eye and mind alike, conscious of the fragmentariness of each 'view', jump backwards and forwards, trying to piece the fragment-views together into a certain whole view of, say, a building or scene. Yet the 'whole view' is only a single view. The mind is too limited to grasp at once all the rich detail of the parts, and the general effect of their relation. It is rather saddening that in his book on *Varieties of Religious Experience*, Professor James never followed out the significance of his principle. For we also are fragments torn out of a whole. What we do with the scene, we do with our lives. The individual self is part of a whole order—of society, of mankind, of a universe; but it has, or consists of, an independent mind and will. It forms its own idea of society and the universe, and its own estimates of value. My will is 'free' in so far as I can and do act on my choice. In one respect my will is not free; my choice cannot be other than mine. Sin is selfishness. We like to use the word of particular kinds of selfishness, those especially to which we are least drawn; but it means only—the self-ness.

'Is that sin?' I called it a *principle* of sin, and we may note three stages.

117

(1) As a principle, the self inevitably affects, in some degree perverts, all we do. Throughout this book, I have been pointing out the evident confusion that we are all seeking an infinite truth and value, but according to the measures of a limited self.

(2) We tend to identify our judgments with the infinite, trying by all sorts of evasions to make the self its own law, which is, however unconsciously, to accept its 'dominion'.

(3) This dominion of the self may be accepted openly and consciously. That is the beginning of wickedness, deliberate and defiant sin. I have traced its beginnings, but I do not need to say much about it. I do not suppose those who love sin will read this book or care for it, but some might who are seeking for another life.

We will only concern ourselves here, therefore, with the first two stages—how the self affects and perverts all we do, and how, in desperation, we try to justify its claims. We dealt with three main things:

(a) We claimed that there is a purpose and a value for life, constituting its importance and meaning. Good—but (1) the moment I grasp a purpose, it is my purpose; its importance is tangled into self-importance; the meanings of life become my meanings, and its ideals are my ideals, and they are different from those of others. I hate self-assertion. Do I hate, can I confess, my own self-assertion? (2) Does not the very importance of the issues involve that I judge other people? Need I remind you again of the psychology of parties? I said a good deal about them.

(b) At least, however, we can set ourselves right. But how can we? We have an immense admiration for a fine character, and for noble personality. Again, that is good, but (1) if we put character-building and the development of personality as aims for ourselves, what is it but self-culture? The end of attainment would be a justified self-admiration. We not only know we never could attain it; the mere thought of it is horrible. Yet (2) people do talk of it, I suppose in sheer desperation. One of the best advertised preachers in London a few years ago said:

'I think there is no more splendid conviction for a man on earth to have than this:

> The one thing I have to grow for God is character — that I may be able to stand and look him in the face and say — I am a worthless servant, I have not done much, but I have brought you a character.' (Guaranteed quotation. Apply R.U.S.I., Whitehall, lxv. p. 529.)

I think that argument has got out of gear somewhere.

(c) Lastly we turned to *Religion*. There is a religious *De Profundis*, a cry of the soul out of darkness to God. It is of that I would speak in the next chapter. It is the sorrow and pathos of our time that we have learnt so much and so fast that this sense of darkness and need has become rather difficult to us. If we take religion positively, as implied by the word experience, that experience is my experience, and God 'is for me' what I experience of him. Where else can I look for God except within, since 'all that is best in me is of God' —according to my judgment of what is best? What have I said except that a good part of me is God—all the God there is 'for me'?

We all recognize the truth of the *De Profundis*, but can we rest in what seems to be a mere negation? The *De Profundis* is a cry, and I have admitted repeatedly that the negations of passivity are no answer to anything. What then are we to do, what can we do, except justify our 'religion' as the expression of the higher self? Here also I give a specimen of the attempt, from Eucken, a very notable pre-war religionist:

The movement towards personality and individualism cannot be regarded as an isolated self-sufficiency (i.e. personal perfection). It must rather mean the winning of a life spiritual in origin, that would fain compass the whole infinitude of Being, draw the world to itself, and fashion it anew from its own centre.

That also seems to have got out of gear. I think it is an exaggeration. I am afraid that we idealists do think that we know (can compass) a great deal more than it is possible we should; we do try to draw the world to ourselves—as much as we can get at—and to fashion it anew from our own centre. That is why we quarrel so much, but, with all our vanity, I do not think we imagine that we can compass and re-fashion the whole infinitude of being. Even the arrangement of eclipses taught us that there are limits to what we can undertake. I am speaking of purely human life and its efforts.

There it all is! Start with the simple activities and purposes, try moral perfection, take refuge in religion—do what one will, seek where one will, go where one will, in full and inevitable circle one comes back to the same point. All down the ages of history, in a thousand ways, man has sought for God, something good beyond himself, true beyond his own thought, but has only found, only can find himself. How could it be otherwise? The self is with you, dominating everything you do, every step of the way.

'Is not the whole thing—religion, life, idealism, everything —a mockery and a farce, a tale told by an idiot?' A vast number of people have said so, and added—'let us eat and drink for tomorrow we die.' You will find Omar Khayyam on the drawing-room table. It is in green morocco. But I think we can say, most of us have said, all that for ourselves. (Green morocco is an expensive binding.) Personally, I would not call life a farce, but many wise men have called it a tragedy. It is an odd thing, but there are men who have faced all this evil in themselves, seen it, put names to it, when we shrank from it and tried to evade it, who yet found an infinite joyousness—'in that evil?' Yes, partly. In life? Yes, wholly, though not always in the parts; some of which remain confusingly nasty. They talked of a thing they called redemption. I will not assume they were wise, but they could not be very foolish if they got this far. Presently I think we might listen to them. They might have something to say.

VI

GOD AND THE SOUL

Iɴ the last chapter, we began with the question: If this is God's world and if there is evil in it, what are we to say? We tried to find out what we meant by evil. We found three sources:

(1) There is evil in nature. Shall we say there is evil in God, or should we say God is an imperfect workman?

(2) Men do evil, and we can explain that as a necessity of free will. But are we to say, can we say, that God is helpless to prevent it?

(3) Lastly, the evil is in me. We have not really touched the matter till we have faced that, since it lies at the root of all the rest; further, I can no longer explain my own evil by the easy argument of 'free will', for I do not will evil. It is just my trouble that my will is not free; it is bound very plainly by its own self-nature, which is not deliberate, and as it were accidental, selfishness; it is an essential and inevitable selfishness—that is, self-ness.

I admit that I have not answered the primary question even now, but at least we have gained a much clearer, a somewhat painfully clear, vision of what the evil is with which we have to deal. We are bound to believe that God is good—all the good there is, not by the accident of his character, but by the very nature and necessity of his being. If, in one way, that adds to our perplexity over evil; in another way, it tallies with what we have found; for if good is not in God, it certainly has no true home in me, in us.

To that I will add a thesis which also is not an answer, but it is a very vital contribution towards whatever answer is possible.

We and all mankind have learnt to *believe* that there was a God, because the world is plainly intelligible, and full of beauty—and that which is intelligible and good can only come from intelligence. We and all mankind have tried to believe *in* God, continued to seek for him, hoped for him, because so much in the world is to us neither intelligible nor good.

If it were not so, we should long ago have forgotten all about God. As in so many religions, the merely good God becomes a name for goodness. You and I give no serious thought to the corporation; for the use of light and water, once they are laid on, depends solely on our choice. Put thus curtly, my thesis may seem a paradox, but, putting it more simply: There is so much intelligence, beauty, and good, that we feel there must be a valid meaning for many things beyond us. We look also to that beyond ourselves for a reconciliation.

The journey 'beyond' is a big venture. Let us see what it involves. We have to live in a world, and our attitude towards it is shaped by two questions.

(*A*) What are we going to do with it?

(*B*) What is it doing, going to do, with us?

We have to deal with both. Even the slacker never simply lets himself drift; at least he tries to pick out the soft things, and shirk the hard ones. To grapple with the world is the way of the hero, as also of the profiteer. Both must face the world as it is, if they are to try what they can do with it, or to get from it. But in all these cases we consider the world as a mechanical order, having mass and energy, which some folks call matter and force. Anyhow it is quite external to ourselves, who, as living souls, compound of intelligence and will, learn how to tear something off it for our own purposes without getting caught and crushed. The world is, as it were, a garden or farm, from which we may get crops according to our skill and energy, if weather and soil permit, for we are not wholly masters; also, by neglect, we may get nothing but thistle-down and nettles.

Suppose now, with this religious instinct, we try to substitute the name of God for that of the world, the questions are as primary as ever but they take on a very new significance. They must be put in a new shape, when instead of a material mechanism, we have to consider our relation to a living Will, which we can no longer assume to be external to ourselves.

(*A*) Plainly we cannot ask what we are going to do with God. We may ask what we are going to do for him. Perhaps we ought to ask first, what does God want us to do.

(*B*) The second question comes in several forms. What is God doing with us? What is God doing through us? What does God do in us?

When we ask these question in relation to the world, the second question—'What does it do?'—was to us energetic people only a necessary starting-point. The first question (*A*) seems the most really important and decisive—'What are we going to do?' In our last chapter we followed that order and we found it full of perplexities and annoyances, as we kept tripping over the self and its self-importance at every turn. Is it not the difficulty of religionism and moralism, that we go on assuming the same order even when we are talking about God? But if we look at our questions, and if we compare them with the experience of our own life, is it not plain that, however of necessity we begin by asking (*A*) what we ought to do, the second set of questions, (*B*) what God does with us, must be in the very nature of things, and is in fact, always final, and at each step decisive?

If we look at these two questions for a moment it is obvious that they correspond to two long-forgotten friends of ours called (*B*) Faith and (*A*) Works.

I am reluctant even to refer to such worn-out orthodoxies, partly lest it should seem I was working to a predetermined conclusion; partly just because the ground is so boggy with pools of controversial ink, and we are tired of getting our boots wet. We have done so much floundering ourselves; what, indeed, does mankind, what do you and I, ever do, except flounder through? You can tell by the stars when you are altogether losing direction, and their reflection will often warn you of the worst pools, but we can only find our way through, out of, round, our own difficulties. It is something to know that others have been there before us. There is a path, and if you and I cannot simply follow the old track— you seldom can in this sort of country—at least we might find bits of it helpful.

Being what we are our first question still is—What are we to do? I remember hearing that a man called Saul, from Tarsus, once asked that question, and some years after a certain jailer asked it of him. The answer was, in both cases, concerned with belief and baptism, neither of which is exactly a matter of doing something. However, there was plenty to do afterwards—so there is for us.

But are we asking our question in a purely personal sense— as it concerns our own duty in life? Possibly that is uppermost in our mind, but at least a good many of us are much more concerned over God's dealings with the world. What is God trying to do? What is God doing with the world? Why is it thus as it is? Why cannot we know? If we did, we would find out quickly enough where to take our place. This eager demand is natural, and I think right. That our inner soul makes it so vehemently shows how very little that self-centred, anti-cosmological, religionism of Ritschl and Harnack corresponds to our real needs.

To know God's ways—what he actually is doing; to know God's purposes—the aim he has in mind, is to know infinite truth and eternal value. Why cannot we know them? I believe there is an answer even to that why, but have we considered what the infinite truth means—as to mere fact, as to what I called mechanism? I have spent a few odd hours, one time or another, poring over rotten chunks of elm, oak, fir; wondering over the mystery of their structure, the lines of growth, the cross-graining—annular and radial; the varieties of decay—life struggling with life. There are apparently many kinds of germs; some marking off their territory with a sharp black line, like a frontier; some clean and wholesome; some poisonous and smelly. If you want to learn, you can begin with a cheap book on Histology (plant-physiology), and go as far as you like or can. I did not get very far and have forgotten most of it, but it opened my eyes to things, and I go on learning and wondering. I read somewhere of a biological student who did five years' research work at three universities on a single muscle in the hind-leg of a frog. Then he stopped; of course, he had not finished. Whatever you want to know, you can mostly get on the road, and go up it till you stop, but you never will finish. The road stretches to infinity.

When you turn from mechanism to purpose, from studying the 'how' to asking about 'why', the result is somewhat different. A few little answers you can get without much difficulty. These logs are for my fire, and rotten wood, if you can get it dry, makes a good blaze. Also wood decays as it reverts to the soil, and to the atmosphere. I might call the one a domestic, and the other a front-garden reason. If, however, you are asking after Ultimate good or purpose—why do things decay? I am an oldish man myself and interested.

This time the answer has no beginning, or it begins at the end. The moment you step outside your own front-gate, you do not find a road stretching to infinity, you tumble into the infinity of the universe straightaway. It is all so impossible, so vast, and so unalterable. Shall I say with Pascal, saint and mathematician—'The infinite silences of space terrify me?' Or, can we bring ourselves to worship? With that question, all the history of man, and all the story of the soul, is one long 'agony', which is Greek for a struggle. So far as mere truth goes—as in natural science—we may worship sheer truth; partly, because nature plainly is ruthless whatever our judgments may be; partly, because, when our scientific friends have put us up to some ingenious dodges, within limits and for a time, the externality of Nature leaves us free to go our own way.

So far then we worship; that is, we submit our judgment patiently to, the truth of things. On the other hand, to say that things are right as they are, involves the surrender of moral existence. The book of Job contains the most complete statement of the contradiction. Job's friends take our quite obvious view that things must be in accord with their (ancient) ethical standards. They definitely reject our modern view of the helplessness of God as inconsistent with all conception of the very meaning of the name. It does not seem to have occurred to them to put God outside the question altogether —Job's wife was the only person who thought of that. It follows that the ethical fault is in Job himself. Job is as certain of the general working of a moral law as the three friends are. He repeats all their theological language, but that general law does not work at all certainly in the particular, and it so happens that we are particulars—individuals. We discussed the personal question, and the world question, separately. Job is vitally concerned with their relations to one another.

Of merely personal pain and loss Job says little or nothing. The sense of wrong, of things having gone wrong, the shame of it—what Hezekiah calls, 'rebuke and blasphemy'—trouble him much more. What he feels most of all is, not so much that it is unreasonable, as that it is unreasoned. Something has happened. Anyone can make an explanation—several explanations—but what happens offers no explanation of its own. To interpret Pascal, it is not the vastness, but the silence of the spaces which is so terrifying. And the reply of Jahveh in the last chapters is just that which I have given. We cavil at 'sheer omnipotence' as an answer. But the reply is less an appeal to omnipotence than to primary causality, to creatorship, and Job so recognizes the open fact that the infinity of ultimate purpose, of true value, is wholly beyond our measure, though it is always intruding into things which we do and must measure.

I said at the start that in religion men had found where the answer to the problem of life lay. I hope I have made it fairly plain in various ways that, nevertheless, religion, just because it is a human effort, cannot find the answer; Job was adjudged 'right' because he had realized that there could be no answer within our measure; but he has, at least, learnt to understand what this question involved far better than we, who like Job's friends, have only blinded our eyes by thinking we can answer; better even than the author of Ecclesiastes, who, lacking Job's trenchant courage in challenging the question, is rather inclined to rest in the admission of contradictions.

As a mere fact our first difficulty is, then, that we have no means in the least adequate to the knowledge of ultimate values. But there is a second and very much greater difficulty. I will put it as a question. Do we want to know these ultimate and true values? There is more than one 'we' in this matter, and they answer differently. The rotter, quite emphatically, does not want to know. The anti-idealist affirms that ultimate values cannot be known, but he affirms it so contemptuously that, on my way of taking such vehemence, I suspect he is afraid such ultimate values are much more real than he cares to think.

I believe everyone feels that the book of Job gives an amazingly frank and true statement of the facts of life. It does not claim to do more than indicate the road up which the answer lies. That is all I ever claimed and all I think it possible to claim for 'Religion'. If you do not care for this road, you must leave things where they are; some people prefer it that way. There are plenty of people bidding you give up the riddle. We would not heed them if there were not so much in ourselves which wanted to forget it, to push it on one side, that we might be free to enjoy ourselves in our own fashion. Frivolity is only a form of swearing at God, or things-in-general. Someone gave it as a typical English-man's sentence: 'It's a fine day. Hang it all! Let's go and kill something.' There are many things you can kill—time, for instance; also your own soul.

If, on the other hand, you are willing to go on, your soul, every soul, must make its own journey. I am not trying to put words in your mouth. Yet you, I too, are only single souls, a little bit isolated by our own perplexities. There is, as I imagine it, a Dialogue of the Soul with God, more or less common to all mankind, as it cries out of the dark to God:

'Lord, why have you made me thus?'

And there is an answer given to all—'Beloved, I made you for myself.'

'But why am I in the dark and in confusion?'

'Beloved, you are in the dark and in confusion, because

129

you are seeking for light and wisdom in yourself. You will not find them there.'

'But why cannot I know what you are doing?'

'Because that is part of a whole universe of meaning, and you cannot know universes. You want to be a God—a Lord of the world—when you are only a little self and my child.'

'But would you have me placid and content?'

'I made you for hope, desire, effort, progress, in order that you might learn. I would have you content with nothing; for content, placidity, quietism, indifference, are the substance of death—except one content, and that is beatitude, content to be small, content to be my child.'

'Can I do nothing?'

'You can do a great many things; then you will help others. And a great many things you cannot do; then others will have to help you, though you will not like it.'

'What can I do? How am I to know?'

'That I shall not tell you. You must use your own judgment, make your own mistakes, and go on trying. You will fail at a lot of things, and that you will like still less.'

'How can I find God?'

'Beloved, you cannot find me, but I have found you.'

'If I cannot find God, how can I come to love him?'

'Love is not a thing you do or come to. It comes to, overcomes, you. Realize this first, that your life is in my hands, not your own; accept it so, and where faith meets hope, love is born. Believe this first, that God so loved his world that he sent his only begotten Son into the world, that you might live through him, and that the cosmos through him should be saved.'

VII

THE GOSPEL

ALL human life is a dualism, made out of contradictory principles. In the end there is a single dualism, of which the two elements are set out in our last two chapters. I state it here as a final result:

There are two things, by each of which your life is being in different respects ruled; either of these you may take as the object of your love, belief, following, and worship—God and yourself.

Stated thus simply, the choice men ought to make is so very obvious that all we religious people assume we have made it. The choice we can make is quite another matter. Can the Self choose God? It has tried to often. Eucken explains the process; St John gives the result: 'the Light shines in darkness, and the darkness did not comprehend it' ('compass' or 'absorb' it). We have been trying to face all this, and the words with which our last chapter ended have brought us to the answer. No answer can be found in our idealisms; for they are our own. No answer can be found in anti-idealism; for that is a despair of all answers. The answer cannot be something which comes from, and thereby is the expression of, ourselves. It must be something which comes *to* us; a Gospel which is preached to us, and preached to all.

All possible faith for man can have but one beginning—'I believe in God, the Maker of heaven and earth,' and this earth God has made mostly out of common-place things, and for mostly common-place people. No doubt there is a great deal of use for people with special capacities and all that sort of thing, but I reckon God's best love is for comfortably stupid people—seeing what a lot of us he makes. I am in love with this Gospel, and I want you to see why we stupid people want it so badly, and what we want it to do for us.

A very dear old Father visited us from America, and I said to him: 'Come, and I will show you my proofs of the existence of God.' (What I actually said was 'proofs of the Resurrection.' When I come to talk of the Gospel, we shall see presently the significance of that difference of phrasing.) Then I showed him our pigs. I love pigs. They are so delightfully ugly, and so blissfully self-satisfied over it. A fat old sow came slowly waddling towards us, with its two huge ears—like Macbeth's dagger—pointing the way that she should go. And the good Father looked puzzled. 'Oh, yes,' I replied, 'if I had shown you stars, flowers, a sunset, you would have said, "Ah! how true!" but I do not greatly need God in order to see that beautiful things are beautiful, and—well—elevating. I do want to hear of a God who can find a beauty and a joy and an eternal value in my poor pigs. If God also laughs softly over their funniness, I do not mind that. I do it too.'

There is a middle-West farmer, a rough chap, who smokes amazingly strong tobacco; I do not like to think he does not appreciate a prairie sunset, but his business in life is pigs. Grossly material no doubt, but God understands him—and the tobacco—and the pigs—and is interested in them all, even in Chicago prices, not only in the thing he might call his soul and its ethical standards—if he ever does call them that. And, as it happens, it is that middle-West farmer, not the New York highbrow, who representatively constitutes America. In the early days of I Samuel I hear that some simple-minded people thought that God would, of course, know where their donkeys had got to, and that perhaps a prophet of God would be able to tell them. The prophet, as it happened, had something to say about kingship, but he put them right about the donkeys first.

All this problem of the self, with its immense pretensions, and the paltriness of its pigs and its donkeys, is to me a very personal question. It is not that other people are absurd and futile, but that I am, and that I cannot get out of it. Am I to accept a life without sincerity in a world without meaning? But what sincerity is possible when I must do something, and yet understand neither the world's meaning nor my own? There seems to me but one alternative—question or hope. Is there a God who understands that bundle of incompetence and commonplace, ugliness and self-satisfaction, which make the most obvious 'experiences' of the sublime thing I call my personality? Can he make any use or sense of it, even if he smiles a bit over its funny absurdities as I like to think he did over the pigs?

What follows are mere orthodoxies, which I kept back till we were sure we wanted them. You may call it a defence of orthodoxy, but what I mean to do is to preach a Gospel, and a Gospel for common people. And I start my orthodoxies with the 'Athanasian Creed', which is the most discredited of all orthodoxies. Be that as it may, it also starts from just this ground:

> Whoever wants to be saved, the first need is that he should hold fast the Catholic Faith, and the Catholic Faith is this that we worship one God in Trinity.

I paraphrase it thus:

(1) The New Testament word 'salvation' means wholeness, or health, a certain necessary rightness, like being on the right road. (It has no direct connection with 'getting into heaven.')

(2) This necessary rightness is Catholic, the same for everybody. Development, progress, how much you make of it, is, of course, different with different people.

(3) It consists in faith in God, and the Creed defines faith, not as holding opinions, metaphysical or other, but as the worship of, a looking up to, God—the Father, the Son, and the Holy Ghost.

Later on, it says that God is uncreated, incomprehensible (in Latin unmeasured, or uncompassed), eternal, omnipotent.

What I have said, what the Athanasian Creed gives, is not so far a Gospel. We believe and we have good reason to believe, that we are God's children; even in this baffling confusion of personality, we are his workmanship. We believe —at least this is our hope—that he understands us, but if I can say that he does understand us, why is it that we cannot understand him? What does God want or mean? What is God doing, or going to do? We had these questions in the dialogue. We have yet to see how faith has been made possible.

It is not merely a question of ignorance. I have more than once affirmed that, while the soul longs for God, the God the self chooses is a self-chosen God. God himself—in plain fact—we do not want.

That is such a very difficult doctrine that it will be a little easier if I take first the case of the prophets, of whom there has been a fair number. We admit regretfully that today there is rather a shortage in the article, but why is it that, keep centenaries (or build tombs) as we will, prophets nearly always have been killed?

Let me tell a little story. Macaulay, comparing Wesley with St Francis, remarked how the Church of England made a schism where Rome made a saint. Being an Anglican, I do not like the remark, but I will not argue. All the same, Macaulay's ignorance was rather pathetic. Rome made a schism out of Waldo, out of St Francis' most devoted followers, out of Savonarola, out of Luther. If St Francis had lived, I hardly see how he could have missed the same fate. He died protesting desperately, but, since he was dead, they built the great church of Assisi for his tomb.

But this is not peculiar to Rome. In Macaulay's own day Wesley came back to Oxford. By some unfortunate blunder the name over his door was 'J. H. Newman'. Of course, Newman was not the same as Wesley; the message was different, and it was a message Macaulay much disliked—as he would have disliked Wesley's for that matter. So Macaulay threw stones with the best of them. 'Oh, for a real prophet—then those other people would hear some home truths they could not shirk.' But prophets will not take up authorized programmes. They have a disastrous habit of shifting questions round in a fashion which brings us all under fire. I can only know they are true prophets if they speak the truth; if one says what I firmly believe to be false, what else can I say except that he is a false prophet. 'Abraham is dead, and the prophets are dead'—for our peace of mind, and for their own safety, they had best stop so.

Is it different with God? We all love God and we cry to God—yes, up in heaven, which is the proper place for archetypal ideas (*see* Plato), and other matters of aspiration. If God takes to walking about on earth, archetypal ideas are all very well, but where do I come in, and what is going to happen to my ideas? It is written that when Adam (Hebrew for Man) and Eve heard the voice of God walking in the garden in the cool of the day, they ran for it. However, they learnt something which they used; for next time men found God in a garden, somewhat late at night, they crucified him in sheer desperation. What else could they do?

'I, if I be lifted up, will draw all men unto me,'—and he

135

did. The common crowd—the herd, as it might be you and me—shouting 'Crucify'; the High Priests, dogged and argumentative; the religionist Pharisees, disapproving the rough secular fashion of it, but glad of the result, at a safe distance; the civil power, puzzled but authorizing; the plain soldiers, carrying out orders; two criminals, one repentant and one unrepentant, the one on his right hand, the other on his left, where two apostles had asked to be; the disciples who fled: one came back, and the Mother—they are all in place round the Cross. And there were some other women. I do not know how they do it, but some always manage to get there.

So things are with us always. Intellectually, truth is never a thing you come to—not by fifty-five years at thirty-three universities. Yet it is always coming to you. Sometimes in comfortable little bits, in response to what you do in the effort of your seeking; quite often, it thrusts its most dis-comfortable bulk into your life, very much un-sought, but always on the point of what happens. Morally, can you come to righteousness by self-seeking? Certainly by no religious effort can I come to God. I can only judge by what appears to me, and choose by what appeals to me. The self cannot go outside the self. Thereby its in-sufficiency cannot be other than a self-sufficiency—separated and alienated from God.

But is God truth? Can God come to me? If I am alien from God, is God alien from me? Sheer despair cries out at it. The modern religious sentiment protests. I would listen to the pleading of despair sympathetically, though I would not trust it for wise answers. Modern sentiment is much less convincing. I asked long ago—'Is God niceness?' One answer is clear—God is truth, and recognizes his own facts. Alienation, so far as it is a feeling, may be on one side only; separation, if it exists in fact, it exists for both. Can God come to me? Of course, in one sense, he is always doing it; that constitutes what God does with you. But if you mean God himself, in such sense that there is real unity between us, so long as I am what I am, an independent and self-acting entity, I do not see how any amount of good-natured niceness on God's part could make it possible.

But there were some wise men—I thought they seemed so—who 'talked of a thing they called Redemption,' which I have been told means a deliverance. Being what we are, can God redeem this self-separation? I do not know; I only know I cannot. There is a hint of real significance as the pronoun changes from the common 'we' to the individual I. What I do, being mine, separates me from other individuals, no less than from God. When I try to help others, there is at once a division, often sharply resented, between the would-be helper and the ought-to-be helped. But what God does, this at least might be common to us all, might constitute a unity, a 'communion', between us.

And these wise men of mine said that this Redemption was not a philosophy, nor a morality, nor a religion; not a way of thinking, acting, or feeling, though all these might grow out of it. Primarily it was a story of what happened, in the fashion truth does come. They called it a Gospel, a story, a message of good-telling. It began in many ways. To some other wise men it began when they saw a star in the East; and to some simple men it began from a vision of angels, and they said, 'Let us now go and see this thing which has happened.' Put very shortly—it concerns one Jesus Christ, the only begotten Son of God, God from God, who being in the form and of the substance of God:

For us men and for our salvation
    Came down from heaven,
And was incarnate by the Holy Spirit of the Virgin Mary
    And was made – man.

He was crucified also for us under Pontius Pilate.
 He suffered and was buried.
And the third day he rose again,
 According to the Scriptures;
He ascended into heaven,
 And sitteth on the right hand of the Father.

Some people believe this story, and some do not. Quite a large number, at all times, have been unable to see any point in what happened, or what difference it is supposed to make even if it were true. On the other hand, I heard of an old corporal in the war, who had been grousing at 'religion', and, on being told this story, replied, 'I wish I could believe it, but it's too good to be true.' What you find in this story will depend on what you are looking for. I have given my own notion of what questions life throws up at us—questions which philosophy, science, progress, are always re-shaping, perhaps making more acute. I am not going to defend this story, but we might ask what those who handed it on to us believed to be its essence. We need not concern ourselves here with the different attempts they made to explain it. If we get the substance of the story right, we may be able to see why they found such an immense joy in preaching it, and handing it on.

About one thing these preachers, or traditionalists, were were quite clear. It was a story about God—that or nothing. There are people who like saint-worship; there is today a very popular cult of heroes and personalities. Possibly, as the story of a quite unique saint, this story may, for anything I know or care, remind such people how they also can make their lives sublime. But there are a great many common people very conscious of their own smallness and futility. There are not a few of us, big or little, quite conscious of the absurdity of their own self-importance, who, with an utter horror of their own craving to be sublime, yet feel bound to follow their 'ambitions'. Some of us are already discouraged by failure and disillusion, and still more by the dread of failure. What Gospel is there for us in a story of virtues we do not possess, achievements we cannot make, and sublimities we are only too fond of imagining for ourselves?

It is very often taken as the story of a heaven-sent, perhaps 'divine', teacher of a new ethical standard. But one had always understood that ethical standards belonged to a law, and that a law is not a gospel. A new standard may be, it seems to be found, quite useful for judging other people, but, on the personal side, there is an uncomfortable feeling that one has already got more ethical standards than one can quite live up to.

'A story about God'—it is not a revelation of what God is like, nor of God's character, which in other words might mean, a dramatic picture of the nature of ultimate ideals. There was an ancient writer who said: 'My soul is athirst for God, yea, even for the living God.' I do not remember that he said: 'for correct information as to God's character.' What Gospel is there, and what redemption, in pictures and visions of that from which I remain in my own self isolated?

Some folk say the creeds want re-stating. Yes, it is often well to try to put a thing in your own words. The creeds themselves are a restatement. What these preachers of a Gospel did think they had to hand on may be put thus:

'You, we, all mankind, have been thinking and dreaming about God, wondering what he was like in just that way; asking, more wisely, what God is doing; and you are weary, because none can answer—neither break the seals nor even look thereon. And we also cannot tell you, but we can tell you what God has done.

'God, God himself, through whom the worlds were made,

from whom is the whole power and purpose of the universe, took into himself, not some great personality, but our common humanity according to its commonness. The Infinitude of Being our littleness would fain compass, and that is, in fact, the uttermost reach of human folly. But that Infinitude, who encompasses all our littleness, united that littleness to himself by the uttermost love of the eternal wisdom.'

Well, I have re-stated it, but one early preacher, not, I am told, of the very earliest, states it much better:

> That which was from the beginning,
> That which we saw with our eyes (apostles),
> And our hands handled
> Concerning the Logos of Life,
> Declare we unto you also (strangers, Englishmen),
> That ye may have fellowship with us (sharing, commonness. I do not know how to translate *Koinonia*),
> And our fellowship is with the Father,
> And with his Son, Jesus the Christ.

I have written these words as if they were a song, according to the rhythm (I can only hope I have got it right). I have not much perception of literary form, still less of music, but I want to sing them; they sing themselves. The splendour of these passages does not lie in the wording and phonetic values. It is the splendour of the substance which gives to the wording also a splendour, which some people do not seem to recognize, I think, because the meaning does not appeal to them.

It is very wonderful, but the glory of it is a little blinding. God came—God took—took our limitations—took that which is common—unity between us and God—thereby a unity amongst ourselves—I see, or I see hints of, these essential points. But what then? 'God took'—What did God do with it? Is the story quite complete? I miss the word Redemption. I can see the meaning is there, plainly there, but

I do not quite see how to fit it in, and it is much too vital to leave in doubt.

No! so far we have had only the beginning. The centre of the story is the crucifixion, and upon the meaning of our life it is wholly central.

> God, who in sundry times and in divers manners,
> Spake in time past unto the fathers by the prophets,
> Hath in this last of days spoken unto us by his Son,
> Whom he established inheritor of all things.

'Spoke'—this is not a 'Dialogue of the Soul with God.' It is an utterance from God to all mankind, yet I will try to give it as a message to the soul, as some have entered into it.

We are wrestling with the confusions of life, and our life is confused, because it is concerned with the eternal and yet is only a temporal fragment. To see life whole you must see it in God where it is a whole, but then the fragment cannot comprehend the whole, nor yet God. Life is shown to you in the wholeness of its true nature, and you can see it, by seeing what happened when God took it. The answer is given in the vision, the story, of a happening—with all the infinity of meaning which belongs to a fact; not in a statement or explanation, with the limited fragmentariness which belongs to explanations.

In the crucifixion, every factor of life, every contradiction, opposition, dualism, can be found. God and man—perfect God, in the fullness of the Divine Substance; perfect Man, of a reasonable soul and human flesh subsisting. Man by himself, of all the different mentalities men have (I said so much of that above); Man, as he is in union with God—natural and super-natural; the material and spiritual—it must never be forgotten that the Cross itself is two rough planks of the commonest wood that could be gotten. (There is even a

significance in the shape, for the two planks go cross-wise—
as material things have a habit of doing.)

Do you enquire further? Name what you like. Authority
and freedom; democracy and autocracy; predestination and
free-will; the things of God and the things of Caesar; social-
ism and individualism (any more?)—if you want controversial
weapons, you may interpret to suit your case; if you want to
understand, you may look and look, pray and ponder, to see
how each shows itself and what each does. Everything *is* there;
it is an at-one-ment of them all.

Do you understand the at-one-ment? Of course not—at
least, not in the sense of 'comprehending'. What I am saying
is that in the crucifixion all these are comprehended, included,
brought together, at-one-d. You and I and the theologians
will try to learn what we can as we need it. I am going on to
that here. (May I repeat? The infinity of truth, of fact, is
always beyond explanation or estimate. If you want to know
what 'love' is, look at mothers, and their children. Any of
them you may see; sometimes by what they are doing, better
by what they are suffering; sometimes by what they are miss-
ing. Do not ask them for an explanation of what love is, for
they cannot tell you, nor can I; nor can you tell them. I only
said you can see—according to your insight.)

You want to do, mean to do, big things. Stick to it! There
are a good many big things, and even the little things are big
some ways, at least if they are worth doing at all. You will
do a good few miracles, my beloved—if God is nice to you
—but Christ did a great many. You would like to be a great
teacher, but 'no man ever talked like this man.' Yet the
apostles say nothing of his miracles, and hardly anything of
his teaching. The key of the whole story is the Cross, and
on the Cross Christ himself does nothing, and says next to
nothing. What is done is done to him; he just suffered. What

is said, mostly is said about him, but he makes no answer. Men challenge him to do something, offer him their faith, offer him victory, if he only will. But that is not what he is after, nor the victory he will win.

We are talking of redemption, and that means an at-one-ment (I do wish we English folk could learn to pronounce that word properly). It means a unity, first between God and man; then, it is a unity also between men; it is one and the same for the builder's labourer and the philosopher, the pig-farmer and the artist and the saint. But what is redeemed? The self is not really at-one with anything: 'neither indeed can be.' It is just *me*. Except so far as the self finds an at-one-ness, satisfying and up-lifting, in that private horizon-world which with placid indifference submits to being thus contemplated. And it is the same with all those activities which are born of the self. My notions, ideals, actions, are just mine. Upon everything I can get at to do, see how busy I am inscribing 'Ego, Me, did it and fixed it.' (That is not correct Latin, but it is the correct meaning.) Do these achievements want redeeming? Personally, I smirk over them. Verily they have, they are, their reward. One does not ordinarily condole with the batsman over the laborious self-sacrifice by which he piled up a century. Certainly to make a 100 will require a great deal of self-sacrifice, not, however, in making those big hits which the ground applauds, but in not hitting many balls he longed to hit, and while the crowd accepts the self-restraint, they are rather bored by it. So far as our achievements and activities go, like our intentions and motives, they remain ours. However well-meaning, they partake of that separation and independence of the self, which is of the very definition of sin—not the deliberate separation which defies God, yet it is separation in fact.

We must put the activities of the self on one side, and try

to understand at least the meaning of the word suffering. Of course, my mind, my attention, is absorbed over what I have chosen to do, want to do—like writing a book. Doing (action) is, therefore, a joy, 'nice'. What happened to me in the past, I have mostly forgotten or take for granted. Other things keep happening, which I have to put up with or suffer. Some of them are quite nice; but as they are not, as they interrupt, what I want to do, mostly they are annoying, 'nasty'. Thus, 'to suffer' is generally used of what is painful though properly it is only the opposite of 'to do'. Forgotten or resented, however, what happens to you, what you suffer, is (1) much the larger and more important part of your life; (2) it is that which belongs to, joins you on to, the common life of men.

A true thinker writes a book in his own markedly personal language, which is, in fact, only a variation of what you and I learnt when we were just out of our cradles. 'But the ideas at least are original.' Are they? Of course, both the language and ideas must have something original, or the book would not be worth writing; if they were wholly original, the book would not be readable. The Bible and Shakespeare—if you understand them and they appeal to you, it is because the Bible is saying what all mankind has been longing to say; and because Shakespeare is saying what you have often tried to say.

All that you and I have thought or done comes in the main from what has happened to us, from what we have suffered, in the common life we share, only in some degree modified by the personal element. And whence it comes, thither also it must return. If it is to live, it must sink into the common possession of mankind, and thereby cease to be yours. As the scientist and engineer run their calculations up and down, few think of or even know who invented the decimal notation or the algebraic symbols, which even a schoolboy handles so easily. 'That which thou sowest is not quickened except it die, and thou sowest not that body which shall be, but God giveth it a body as it hath pleased him.'

And now, what does happen to us? What is it to suffer? Our life is so small, so fragmentary, so full of contradiction, and we are so helpless. It is only to our vanity that it seems complete, and to our ambition that it seems so important. What happens to you is always failure and disillusion—that is, if you have understood it. It is only in the paltriness of melodrama that everybody marries, and 'lives happily ever after.' Pitch your aims small as you may, what will happen to you is suffering, and in the end death. In these the dumb life acquiesces unquestioning, wholly in the vegetable, with only a moment's instinctive resistance in the animal; against these the intelligent self is always and of necessity in revolt. Whether such things are really evil or not, to its judgment they must be. 'But what God chose, that God redeemed,' and it is just these which God chose; it is just that which seems farthest from the divine nature, which God reconciled to God.

> Not by conversion of the Godhead into flesh,
> (not by making God weak and passible),
> But by taking of the manhood into God.

The crucifixion, then, I call the centre, the subject, of the story. The climax or end of it you know—He rose again from the dead, and ascended into heaven. It is this end which alone makes it a story of good, of joy and hope. In English 'Gospel' is only a noun, and our English Bible uses 'to preach' where the New Testament says 'to gospel', i.e. 'to tell the great story'. St Luke gives the substance of some of St Paul's sermons; more frequently he just gives its central point. There seem to have been three main points of this preaching:

(1) Jesus is the Messiah (the Christ); (2) the Messiah must suffer; (3) Jesus and the Resurrection. The significance of the first we will consider presently. The second we have just considered. Now we will take the third.

No one, I believe, doubts that St Paul regarded the Resurrection as the very substance of the Gospel. But, as a dear brother of mine once put it—'Some folk seem to think Christianity was a very beautiful thing till St Paul came and spoilt it'; though, as regards the broad issues, St Paul, St Peter, St John, and the Epistle to the Hebrews are all at one. The Synoptic Gospels, however, except in certain apparently added verses or chapters, seem curiously reticent, even perplexed, over the finish of the story. It has been suggested that perhaps it did not belong to the earliest tradition. But here I should like to say something about Bible interpretation. When our early Victorian ancestors wanted to prove something, they used to cite texts. Then their opponents cited other texts, which was puzzling. When modern scholars want to prove, or to disprove, something, they reconstruct documents, and other scholars reconstruct them differently, which is much more puzzling. I do not know much of New Testament criticism. A good deal of it, I have not brains enough to follow or remember. Certainly I am much too ignorant to discuss it.

As a common person, when I am asked Bible authority for anything worth arguing about, I learnt from Maurice to quote 'In the beginning God created the heaven and the earth', down to 'even so, Come Lord Jesus', and every single verse betwixt and between. Anything which is there at all, is there in every verse, for the story is, and always has been, a whole. The Church might read selections in bits, but the service (liturgy) itself was a memorial of the Passion, and Sunday was the festival of the Resurrection. Just now, however, let us take St Mark, and admit that the last page has disappeared at 16.8. Very well, as evidence for the Resurrection I quote all that is left, from the first verse:

> The beginning of the Gospel
> Of Jesus Christ, the son of God,

all down—through Peter's wife's mother and the rest—up to:

> And they said nothing to anyone
> For they were frightened.

What is it *all* about? A story of a man of remarkable powers (an early Coué?) and remarkable sayings who got killed? Why call it a Gospel? Parts of it are pathetic, and parts fantastic, and the whole more than a bit futile. The Gospel narratives show, were intended to show, how perplexing our Lord's life was to his disciples; when the Resurrection did come, how staggered they were at it. Nevertheless, the narrative was, and only could have been, written under the consciousness of this climax, in the glory and faith of the apostolic Gospel. Certainly there is a contrast, but the evangelists did not see any inconsistency between the perplexity of the early and the glorious confidence of the later time. They believed they were showing how the one was transfigured into the other, just as the apostles believed that they were showing how we might be delivered out of the power of darkness (which is the contradictions of this life) and translated into the kingdom of the Son of his love.

For years the disciples had had the companionship and teaching and direct influence of what we call—and they felt to be—a unique or radiant personality. 'We hoped it should have been he that would have redeemed Israel, but our rulers delivered him up and crucified him. And there are certain women of ours—and a vision of angels—and it is all very staggering.' And then—a few weeks—in their sight he went up from them into heaven. There is no mistaking that. All that they had loved and enjoyed and valued is gone finally, and, just because it is gone, at once, quite suddenly, the door opens into a new life. The personal and temporal, the very attraction of which had somewhat blinded their eyes—as it is apt to blind ours—was only a veil. Now that it is drawn aside, they realize that what had been given them was a Gospel of God, universal and eternal. They go back rejoicing, and act with the confidence of an assured understanding (Acts 1.14 to end). Only ten days later St Peter states the principle. The crucifixion, though done by the hands of lawless men, was of the determinate counsel and foreknowledge of God.

This is the meaning of the first of St Paul's three essential points—that 'Jesus is the Messiah.' The Gospel of one Jesus, what he did and what men did with him, is no surprising incident—like the emergence of a St Francis—it was purposed in Christ Jesus, according to an eternal purpose hidden in God, kept in silence before the foundation of the world, before times eternal. The world was created, man was created, just thus-wise for redemption according to the good-pleasure of him who worketh all things according to the pleasure of his will. Wherefore the Lord himself, 'beginning from Moses and all the prophets, interpreted unto them the Scriptures', and so St Paul. There is a promise to Adam, and to Noah, and to Abraham.

I will not hunt for specially Messianic texts. Here are two verses from I Chron. 2.39: 'And Azariah begat Helez, and Helez, Eleazar', and so on to Sismai, and Shallam—about twenty columns—'having a low degree of inspiration.' (I do not know what that means; it is a quotation.) Who are these people, and what are they doing in the Bible? I suppose they were much like the 'Eliud who begat (another) Eleazar, and Eleazar begat Matthan, and Matthan begat Jacob', and there was a Welsh quarry-man, who prayed, 'Lord, thou knowest I cannot make to pronounce these names, so I will call them Williams and Jones and Richards.' An ignorant literalist, yet it is the best commentary I know; for that is just what they do mean, ordinary unseeing people, like you and me. Probably they also had a low degree of inspiration, carrying on as they could while God prepared his time for:

> Jacob begat Joseph,
> The husband of Mary,
> Of whom was born Jesus,
> Who is called the Christ.

Thus, while the Gospel is essentially an eternal Gospel, it is no less essentially the story of an incident in which that purpose was manifested and revealed in its accomplishment. I have liked to remark that 'under Pontius Pilate' is the only entirely novel and original clause in our creeds. You may find parallels in comparative religions, many parallels, to everything else—the Trinity, the Incarnation, the Virgin Birth, the death and resurrection of the God. At least at times men knew their own needs sufficiently to see what God must be, and how he *might* come to men. But 'what men longed to say, they could not'—namely, that he had come. 'Under Pontius Pilate' is only the ancient way of dating an historic fact. It means just this, that God has effected in fact all and more than all man dreamt of, what neither dream nor act nor thought of his could effect, and so it was that:

> Very early in the morning
> The first day of the week
> They came unto the sepulchre
> At the rising of the sun.

And they said:

> Who shall roll us away the stone
> From the door of the sepulchre?

And when they looked,

> They saw that it was rolled away,
> For it was very great.

This question mankind has been always asking, and this, if you will look, you also may see.

Surely this is plain that only facts are common. That was why in my pig story I spoke of proofs, not of the mere existence of God, but of the Resurrection; I might have better said of the Ascension. You cannot make a Gospel out of ideals. Here is a test:

> The sun, the moon, the stars, the seas, the hills, and the
>   plains,
> Are not these, O Soul, the vision of him who reigns?
> And is not the vision he?

The first lines are strictly selective of things great, up-lifting—'numinous' is our latest word—but you cannot put my pigs into it. Ugliness, vulgarity, stupidity, evil, suffering, death, are all very common; we have to face and to deal with them in the world and in ourselves. But we must not make them into ideals. Fried bacon is very nice; I enjoy it, and give God thanks, but the man is a fool who pictures heaven in such ways.

The poem, however, pictures God in terms of ideals. Then the inference of God—given as a question—becomes a specu-lation, and ends as a vision, an experience or phase of feeling, taken as its own object. The vision 'is' God; all there is. And, thereby, we have produced that thrice-deplorable thing—a religion for the religious, in no real relation with the rough-and-tumble life of common people.

Is God more than a vision of mine, or a dream? Can God at-one this broken life of mine? How can I see more than a vision, or think more than my own thoughts? I had heard of God, and my heart awoke, for it might mean so much. But what does God do? I do not know. I do not see how I could know, and the hope dies down. It was then the message came to me. We value St John's Epistle because it contains some remarkable passages on the essential love (the Holy Spirit) who is in God, who is God. But most of that Epistle is about the Incarnation. I gave the beginning before, and this is the end:

> We know that the Son of God is come
> And we are in him that is true,
> Even in his Son, Jesus Christ.
> This is true God, and eternal life.

> Little children, keep yourselves from idols.

I wonder how many stop to realize the tremendous warning in the apparent irrelevance of that last line, which is not part of the rhythm. If you would ever come to truth, that it may ever come to you, this first—you must keep yourself from the worship of your own visions, ideals, experiences. In place of our efforts to apprehend God—not, indeed, displacing them, rather glorifying them with its own light—stands this assurance of a Gospel. You may believe it or not, but there is no other:

> Now is Christ risen from the dead,
> And become the first-fruits
>   Of them that sleep;
> For as in Adam (in man) all die,
>   Even so in Christ shall all be made to live.